TEST SCORES
AND
WHAT THEY MEAN

TEST SCORES
AND
WHAT THEY MEAN

FOURTH EDITION

HOWARD B. LYMAN

University of Cincinnati

Prentice-Hall Englewood Cliffs, New Jersey 07632

Library of Congress Cataloging-in-Publication Data

Lyman, Howard Burbeck, (date)
   Test scores and what they mean.

     Bibliography: p.
     Includes index.
     1. Educational tests and measurements—
United States—Interpretation. 2. Educational tests
and measurements—United States—Validity. 3. Edu-
cational tests and measurements—United States—Data
processing. 4. Psychological tests—United States—
Interpretation. 5. Psychological tests—
United States—Validity. 6. Psychological tests—
United States—Data processing. I. Title.
LB3060.8.L85 1986   371.2′6   85-12415
ISBN 0-13-903832-9

Editorial/production supervision
  and interior design: Marianne Peters
Manufacturing buyer: Barbara Kelly Kittle

Printed in the United States of America

10 9 8 7 6 5 4 3 2 1

ISBN   0-13-903832-9   01

Prentice-Hall International (UK) Limited, *London*
Prentice-Hall of Australia Pty. Limited, *Sydney*
Prentice-Hall Canada Inc., *Toronto*
Prentice-Hall Hispanoamericana, S.A., *Mexico*
Prentice-Hall of India Private Limited, *New Delhi*
Prentice-Hall of Japan, Inc., *Tokyo*
Prentice-Hall of Southeast Asia Pte. Ltd., *Singapore*
Editora Prentice-Hall do Brasil, Ltda., *Rio de Janeiro*
Whitehall Books Limited, *Wellington, New Zealand*

2

2

This
Fourth
Edition
Is Affectionately
Dedicated
to

2,

2

too

2

CONTENTS

PREFACE

This Fourth Edition of *Test Scores and What They Mean* has been made necessary by the constant changes in testing. Testing continues to be a most dynamic field of study!

In the First Edition (1963), I noted that many people have positions that give them access to test results—regardless of their level of knowledge (or ignorance) about tests. Such people include physicians, school teachers and principals, admissions counselors, social workers, and personnel workers. I wrote *Test Scores and What They Mean* for people like these.

It soon became apparent that the book was being used even more frequently as a supplementary text in courses in educational measurement, psychological testing, personnel work, counseling, and so on. I tried to make the Second Edition (1971) especially useful to students of testing.

My goal in the Third Edition (1979) was to update the earlier editions and to make the book even easier to read. Aside from one crank letter that accused me of being a press agent and apologist for the test publishers, the least favorable review came from a professor who wrote to Prentice-Hall complaining that the chapter on statistics wasn't any easier than those in other books. Fortunately some people think otherwise. Most reviewers have remarked that the book is easy to read, full of illustrative anecdotal material, and genuinely informative.

Several test publishers and at least one industrial consulting firm have found the book so useful that they have made it available to their customers. One American test publisher requires all new employees to read the book for general background information. And one English business man who formerly headed a test publisher's office in the U. K. told me, "Frankly, without your book, I wouldn't have known anything about tests!"

I keep up-to-date in testing through reading the appropriate literature, through my teaching, and through my research. Test publishers also help keep me current. They furnish me with copies of tests and related materials; more than that, they are willing to answer questions and to offer advice. I want to thank personnel from: The Psychological Corporation and Harcourt Brace Jovanovich, Educational Testing Service, Riverside Press, American Guidance Services, Consulting Psychologists Press, CTB/McGraw-Hill, Scholastic Testing Services, Institute for Personality and Ability Testing, Research Psychologists Press, Psych Systems, and EdITS (Educational and Industrial Testing Service). As with earlier editions, I have found it more difficult to *select* examples than to *find* examples of tests to use in this Fourth Edition.

My philosophy of testing is still evolving. It has been influenced by the following—people who have taught me both as an undergraduate and graduate: J. McVicker Hunt, Donald Lindsley, Donald G. Paterson, Howard P. Longstaff, C. Gilbert Wrenn, Walter Cook, W. S. Miller, John G. Darley, Ralph F. Berdie, E. G. Williamson, Herbert Sorenson, Robert North, and Lysle Croft. My views also have been seasoned through years of using tests, teaching about tests, and consulting on testing problems with a wide variety of people and agencies.

I want to thank the many readers of the first three editions of *Test Scores and What They Mean*, especially those who were kind enough to share their comments with me. I thank those colleagues and friends who have shared their views on test-related issues with me at one time or another: Goldine Gleser, Venus Bluestein, R. J. Senter, Richard Melton, Earl Kronenberger, Vytautus J. Bieliauskas, Gerald Doppelt, Frank Womer, Joan Bollenbacher, Kenneth McLaughlin, and Peter Merenda.

Although I have written *Test Scores and What They Mean* with American test users in mind, I was pleased to discover that some foreign psychologists and educators have found the book useful. There have been both Japanese and Spanish editions published and, on a recent sabbatical in Europe, I was delighted to find copies of the English-language editions in several libraries. Indeed, I was pleasantly surprised to learn that this book has at least a modest following overseas. (Although it hasn't penetrated far beyond the Iron Curtain, the book was reviewed in at least one Polish publication.)

Additionally I thank the four professional reviewers retained by Prentice-Hall: George Cunningham of the University of Louisville, Louise Fitzgerald of Kent State University, Bruce McDonald of Southern Illinois University, and Philip Smith of the University of Wisconsin-Milwaukee. Their criticisms and suggestions were carefully considered, and many were adopted. A major change in this Fourth Edition includes a shortening of the material on test manuals and profiles (viewed as interesting but too long and too wordy). Additional information (or completely new content) has been given on such topics as:

- Need for competency testing in the schools
- Accountability and responsibility
- Computer-assisted testing, scoring, and reporting
- Need for guidelines in use of computers in testing
- Latent trait test construction
- New growth in performance testing
- Adaptive testing

In addition, of course, I have updated most of the references and the examples used in this book. I hope that you enjoy reading this book as much as I have enjoyed writing it!

1 ‖ INTERPRETING TEST SCORES

"When am I going to start failing?" a student asked me several years ago. Upon being questioned, he told me this story: "My high school teacher told me that my IQ is only 88. He said that I might be able to get into college because of my football, but that I'd be certain to flunk out—with an IQ like that!" I pointed out to Don that he had been doing well in my course. I found out that he had had a B+ average for the three semesters he had completed. I reminded him that the proof of a pudding lies in its eating—and that the proof of scholastic achievement lies in grades, not in a test designed to predict grades.

Last June, Don graduated with honors.

One eminent Black psychologist tells much the same story about himself. Very much a disbeliever in the value of testing—especially for minority youth—he had been told in high school that his intelligence test results were so low that he'd never be admitted to college. Now he has his Ph.D. in psychology.

These two stories illustrate many principles; for example:

Were the test scores correct? Were there errors in administration or in the scoring? Could the scores have been percentile ranks instead of IQs?

Should teachers be so precise in stating scores without giving their respective students a thorough explanation of the tests and the scores obtained?

One shouldn't make such bald assertions about test results; no test score (or any other basis for prediction) predicts perfectly.

No test score determines future performance. Demonstrated performance is better evidence than any test score, as both students proved in their subsequent achievements.

Mistakes in test interpretation occur every day. Here are three more examples that come quickly to mind:

A college freshman, told that she had "average ability," withdrew from college. Her counselor had not added ". . . when compared with students in other topflight colleges." The freshman reasoned that if she had only average ability compared with people in general, she must be very low when compared with college students; rather than face that situation, she dropped out of college. (There may have been other reasons, too, but this seemed to be the principal one.)

A high school student who had high measured clerical and literary *interests* was told that this proved that he should become either a clerk or a writer!

A personnel manager, learning that one of her best workers had scored very low on tests that eventually would be used in selecting future employees, nearly discharged the worker; ". . . the tests really opened our eyes about her. Why, she's worked here for several years, does good work, gets along well with the others. Those tests show how she had us fooled!"

None of these cases is fictitious. All involve real people. And we will see many more examples of test interpretation throughout this book. Each is based on a true situation, mostly drawn from my personal experience in working with people who use tests and who take tests.

No amount of anecdotal material, however, can show the thousands of instances every year in which the wrong persons are selected for jobs, admitted to schools and colleges, granted scholarships, and the like— merely because someone in authority is unable to interpret available test scores or, equally bad, places undue confidence in the results.

Nor will anecdotal material reveal the full scope of the misinformation being given to students and parents by teachers and others who are trying to help. Willingness to help is only the first step. There is also a great deal to know about the meaning of test scores. Even experts who work daily with tests must keep their wits about them, for this is no game for dullards.

TESTING TODAY

The quality of tests has improved greatly since the 1920s. Definite advances in testing have been noted even in the past decade: in novel approaches to achievement testing, in machine-scoring and -interpreting, in varied approaches to the measurement of interests, etc. Most test authors and test publishers are competent and service-motivated; they subscribe to ethical standards that are commendably high. Each year universities turn out greater numbers of well-trained measurements people. More and more teachers and personnel workers are being taught the fundamentals of testing. In spite of these and other positive influences, we still find a desperate need for wider understanding of *what test scores mean*.

More than one million standardized tests per school day are used in American schools alone. Add to this number the tests that are being given in industry, personnel offices, employment bureaus, hospitals, civil service agencies, etc.—add all of these in, and we can conclude that there is a great deal of testing being done.

Who will interpret the test scores? Often, nobody. In millions of instances, test scores never progress beyond a file card or folder; indeed, this has been the official policy of many personnel offices and school systems. In other instances, the scores are made available to supervisors or teachers who may, at their discretion, interpret the results.

Unfortunately, many people whose *positions* seem to give them legitimate access to test results have had little training in test interpretation. People who are going to have access to test scores have an obligation to learn what scores mean; however, many do not even realize the extent of their ignorance. I should not have been surprised at the following incident:

> I was asking about some test scores made by my son David. As an eighth-grader in a large school system, he was in a research study and had taken an extensive test battery. His homeroom teacher, Betty Blenkove, must have been taught that tests should be kept secure; she extracted a key from her handbag, unlocked her desk, took out a ring of keys, selected one, and unlocked a storage closet; from the closet, she drew a folder out from underneath a stack of books. Ms. Blenkove promptly read off a long list of David's scores. "What tests are these?" I asked. She didn't know. "Do these scores compare Dave with the national norms group, the local school norms group, or just those in the research project?" She didn't know. Nor could she tell me anything about other tests that David had taken. She thought the counselor might have that information—or perhaps it was in the principal's office—she wasn't sure.
>
> Ms. Blenkove is a good teacher, and her students like her. But she was taught very little in college about the use of tests, and her work today keeps her busy. Consequently, she finds it easy to pay little attention to standardized tests taken by her students. She reasons that Hallie Halone, the counselor, knows more about tests and will take care of any test interpretation that needs to be done.
>
> Ms. Halone is a certified school counselor. She has had only a little training in tests and measurements because she had to take courses for a teaching certificate before she could start her counselor preparation. She wants to take more courses in measurement, but can't find the time to do so. She tries to see her students as often as she can, but she has nearly 1,000 students to counsel.
>
> As you have suspected, many students are never given much information about their test results. Who has time?

This school system is a good one. Policies are enlightened, and personnel are interested in their students. Testing is not, after all, the school's most important activity. Good tests are selected, administered, scored, and recorded properly; and a few teachers do a remarkable job of using the test results and in interpreting the results to their students. Most do not.

The typical school system has few teachers who are well trained in testing because most teachers have had little opportunity to take elective courses while in college. Many states do not require tests and measurements courses.

Even those teachers who have had a course probably were taught less about what test scores mean and how to interpret test results than they were taught about general principles of measurement and the construction of classroom tests.

Personnel workers in industry often have had no training in tests and measurements. Test interpretation in industry is even worse than in education—except for one thing: industry seldom gives tests for purposes of individual guidance because most tests are used as a basis for institutional decisions. (See below.)

NO MORE STALLING!

Federal law now demands that all schools at all levels as well as all educational agencies that receive federal funds *must* provide freedom of access to student records. Adult students and parents of minor students must be allowed to examine and challenge contents of all school files relevant to the students if they so request. (See Chapter 2.)

All school personnel have an ethical obligation to provide suitable interpretation along with the release of test scores. That in turn means that all school personnel have an additional ethical and professional obligation: to learn about tests and what test scores mean *now*.

Now is the time for learning. No more stalling!

This same warning applies at least equally as well to personnel workers who are concerned with the selection and/or advancement of employees. Federal guidelines set by the Equal Employment Opportunities Commission now require that we all must be able to demonstrate the validity of our selection procedures—including any tests that may be used.

Institutional and Individual Decisions

Tests are often used as tools in reaching decisions. Some decisions are *institutional;* that is, the decisions are made on behalf of an institution (school, college, corporation, etc.), and such decisions are made frequently. Two examples of such institutional decisions are: which persons to select and which to reject and where to place a particular examinee. Tests can be extremely effective in such situations because they help the institution to reach a higher percentage of good decisions. And an occasional bad decision about an individual is not likely to have any adverse effect on the institution. Tests can be used more effectively to predict the performance of a group than they can to predict the performance of an individual.

> Let us test a random sample of 1,000 fifth-grade pupils. Let me have the top fifty pupils, and you take the bottom fifty pupils. You may decide what these 100 pupils are to be taught. You may have a team of experts to help you teach your pupils; I will teach mine myself. At the end of one semester, we will give both groups the same final examination. Regardless of the subject matter taught, I am sure that my group will be higher on the average. *Some* of your pupils may outscore *some* of mine—despite that tremendous original difference in ability. Which of your pupils will show this tremendous response to superior teaching? Which of my pupils will lag far behind the others? We cannot predict accurately which ones these will be; however, we can have considerable confidence in predicting that my group will have the higher average achievement.

A second general type of decision is the *individual* decision. Here, people make decisions that will affect themselves, or perhaps, a son or daughter. The individual has no backlog of similar decisions and may never have to reach a comparable decision again. The situation is unique insofar as the individual is concerned, and a wrong decision may have a lasting effect. Typical examples of individual decisions include whether to accept a certain job offer, whether to go to college, which college to attend, which curriculum to study, which course to take, or which person to marry. Tests sometimes may help, but they are rarely so helpful as in institutional decisions. Tests are far less accurate in individual situations.

A PRETEST

As a pretest of your own ability to interpret test scores, try the following questions—typical of those asked by test-naïve teachers and personnel workers. If you answer the questions satisfactorily (answers at the end of this chapter), you will probably learn little from this book. If you cannot understand the questions, you certainly need this book! Let us see how you do.

1. Why don't we use the raw score itself in test interpretation?
2. What is the difference between a percentile rank and a percentage-correct score?
3. Why are norms important?
4. Do IQs change?
5. What is the difference between reliability and validity?
6. What effect does the range of scores have on test reliability and validity?

7. **Are tests fair to minorities?**
8. **Do tests measure native (i.e., inborn) ability?**
9. **How big must a difference be in order to be called a "significant difference"?**
10. **How can test difficulty influence the apparent performance or improvement of a school class?**

Did you take the pretest? If not, go back and take it now—before reading the answers which follow.

ANSWERS TO PRETEST QUESTIONS

1. Why don't we use the raw score itself in test interpretation?

The raw score, based usually on the number of items answered correctly, depends so much on the number and difficulty of the test items that it is nearly valueless in test interpretation; however, because it provides the basis for all other types of scores, the raw score needs to be accurate. In other words, the raw score is basic—nothing can be more accurate.

There are a few instances in which the raw score does assume greater meaning. For example, in a typing speed test, the score is based on the number of words typed per minute (corrected for errors); that score, itself, is meaningful. And in some respects the scores on other criterion-referenced tests (see Chapter 2) seem to take on more meaning. But these are the exceptions; in most instances we need to go beyond raw scores for meaning.

2. What is the difference between a percentile rank and a percentage-correct score?

A person's *percentile rank* describes relative standing within a particular group: for example, a percentile rank of 80 (P_{80}) means that a person's score is equal to or higher than the scores made by 80% of the **people** in some specified group. A *percentage-correct score,* on the other hand, tells us nothing about a person's relative performance. It tells us only the percentage of **items** answered correctly; for example, a percentage-correct score of 80 means that a person has answered 80% of the test items correctly.

3. Why are norms important?

Norms give meaning to our scores. They provide a basis for comparing one individual's score with the scores of others who have taken the test. Ideally the test publisher describes the norm groups as precisely as possible so that the user may decide how appropriate they are for reporting the performance of individuals of interest. Local norms, developed by the user, may be more appropriate in some situations than any of the publisher's norms. Norms tables are used to translate raw scores into derived scores such as percentiles, standard scores, grade-equivalent scores, IQs, and the like.

4.   Do IQs change?

Volumes could be written (and have been) on this topic. Even under ideal conditions (for example, a short time between testings on the same test for a highly motivated young adult), we would expect to find slight differences in IQ from testing to testing. In general, changes in IQ tend to be greatest in the following situations: among young children, when a long time separates the first and subsequent testings, when different tests are used, when there has been a major change in environmental factors, and when there is a marked difference in motivational level of the examinee at the different test sessions. Changes of five IQ points are common even under good conditions. Rarely will individuals vary so much as to be classified as normal or average at one time and either mentally retarded or near-genius at some other time. The IQ is only a type of test score. Any fluctuation or inaccuracy in test performance will be reflected in the scores and will cause differences in the IQ score.

5.   What is the difference between reliability and validity?

Reliability refers to the *reproduceability* of a set of test results under different conditions (that is, the stability or consistency of scores). *Validity* refers to a test's ability to measure what we want it to. High reliability is necessary for reasonable validity because a test that does not measure consistently cannot measure anything well; however, a test may be highly reliable without being able to do a specified task well.

6.   What effect does the range of scores have on test reliability and validity?

Variability has a great effect on both reliability and validity. Other things being equal, a greater range in scores makes for higher reliability and validity coefficients. The sophisticated test user bears this fact in mind when he reads reliability and validity coefficients in test manuals.

7.   Are tests fair to minorities?

It all depends but, in general, no. All tests are culture-bound to some extent. Most intelligence tests emphasize the sorts of material studied in school; school-related test items are more likely to be familiar to children from upper- and middle-class families. It is possible to construct a test that will result in higher scores for blacks than for whites, but such a test may not reflect the skills and knowledge that most people (especially whites) feel are included as part of intelligence. Any test that is worthwhile must *discriminate;* after all, this is just another way of saying that it will "reveal individual differences." But the intended discrimination should be on the basis of the trait being measured, not on the basis of racial or ethnic background.

8. *Do tests measure native (i.e., inborn) ability?*

Only partly and indirectly. Any intelligence test (or aptitude or achievement test) does measure native ability—but only as it has been modified by the influence of the environment (including all training, experience, and learning), and by the motivation of the examinee at the time he is tested. It is clearly a mistake to think of anyone's IQ as being purely inborn or as being determined solely by heredity; however, it is equally wrong to regard intelligence as determined entirely by environmental factors.

9. *How big must a difference be in order to be called a "significant difference"?*

As we will see in subsequent chapters, there are statistics that give us some idea of how far apart a person's scores must be before we can be reasonably sure that they are truly different; however, no single statistic answers the question simply and satisfactorily in all situations.

10. *How can test difficulty influence the apparent performance or improvement of a school class?*

If a test is far too easy for a class, some pupils will obtain scores that are *lower* than they should be, because we cannot tell *how much better* the pupils might have been able to do if there had been more items of suitable difficulty. If the pupils are given a test of appropriate difficulty some time later, they will appear to have made greater gains than we would expect; now they are not prohibited (by the very content of the test) from attempting items of reasonable difficulty, and fewer students obtain near-perfect scores. There are many other facets to the problem of item difficulty. Some of these will be considered later in this book.

How did you do?

2 ‖ SOME NEW DEVELOPMENTS

The 1970s were exciting years for people who work with tests. The decade was one in which the concept of criterion-referenced testing came into its own. Another impressive development was the passage of federal legislation demanding that schools make test results available to students and/or parents. Even further developments may be expected in the near future, especially in computer applications to testing.

CRITERION-REFERENCED MEASUREMENT

Criterion-referenced testing (also called *domain-referenced* or *edumetric* testing) is not new. Its emphasis is.

> As personnel managers of Jane and Jim Jewelry Manufacturing, we would not be interested in how the typing speed of applicant Dexter Doyle compares with the typing speed of American clerical employees. We would be much more interested in the number of words per minute (corrected for mistakes) typed during a job sample of, perhaps, five or ten minutes.

Although the typing speed test is a common example, it is neither the original use of criterion-referenced testing nor the most prevalent example. Dubois, in his *History of Psychological Testing,* credits the Chinese of nearly four thousand years ago with the first known use of standardized tests. Some of these tests (for example, calligraphy and horsemanship) were almost certainly used as criterion-referenced tests.

Some early tests in this country were criterion-referenced. The *Ayres Handwriting Scale* (in 1912), for example, provided a teacher with a set of penmanship specimens against which to compare each pupil's handwriting. The score was based directly on the quality of the child's performance relative to the quality of the standard specimens; there was no between-pupil comparison involved. *Norm-referenced* tests, on the other hand, base scores primarily on inter-individual comparisons (called Type II scores in Chapter 6).

As adapted to school use, the criterion-referenced test is generally one of a series of coordinated achievement tests that is designed to measure a single behavioral objective within a course of study. Ideally the pupils would have no knowledge of the unit's content before instruction and complete knowledge after instruction. In practice, the teacher strives for pupil *mastery* of the material.

Mastery, though, does not mean complete knowledge of the content; rather, mastery is defined (usually by the test publisher) as obtaining a score of at least 80% (or perhaps 75%) correct.

> One may question how much mastery is involved when one can "pass" by answering fifteen out of twenty four-alternative multiple-choice test items correctly. Yet this assumption is made in many states on driver-license examinations; the applicant can still "pass" when showing false information on 25 percent of the questions about driving laws!

A criterion-referenced approach in teaching involves identifying units of knowledge or skill (much as one would do in developing a program for a teaching machine). One or more tests are used to evaluate pupil mastery of each unit. Only when the pupil has demonstrated mastery (as defined) may the pupil proceed to the next unit of study.

Such an approach is said to encourage greater teacher emphasis on individualized instruction and to enable pupils to work at their own respective paces. The approach allegedly discourages stereotyping individual pupils as *dull* or *slow,* and it clearly discourages comparison of the relative performance of pupils.

The criterion-referenced approach leads to a philosophy that people differ not so much in intelligence as in the speed with which they acquire facts and skills. Presumably the view also helps teachers to be more patient and understanding with pupils who do learn more slowly. Enthusiasts believe that teachers who are more concerned with a *norm*-referenced point of view are likely to neglect slower learners in order to spend more time with average and above-average pupils.

Evaluation of Criterion-Referenced Testing

This reasoning may sound intriguing, but there are limitations. Some edumetric theorists try to give different meanings to validity and reliability (important measurement concepts defined more fully in the next chapter), but this seems wishful thinking; validity and reliability, as the terms are commonly used, are still important. The major test publishers do pay attention to these concepts, but some tests produced by new publishers are atrocious—particularly in their use of shockingly few items.

Those who want further information about criterion-referenced testing should read Marion F. Shaycoft's *Handbook of Criterion-Referenced Testing* (Garland STPM Press, 1979). She shows that it is perfectly possible for the same test to be *both* norm- and criterion-referenced. Although some of the reading is highly technical, much of the book requires little sophistication in the field of testing.

Accessibility of Test Results

Test results must be made available to school students and/or their parents. That is one of the effects of a federal law passed in 1974. Every school (from nursery school through graduate and professional schools) and all educational agencies that receive any funds from the federal government must make available to parents of minors ". . . any and all official records, files, and data directly related to their children. . . ."

I regret this practice had to be mandated by the government, but I am delighted that students and their parents are able to learn how they performed on the tests they have taken. Even before the law became effective, test publishers had been taking steps to encourage accurate and effective interpretation of test results.

EQUAL EMPLOYMENT OPPORTUNITIES COMMISSION

The EEOC is a federal watchdog charged with responsibility for insuring fairness in the selection of people for employment. The law demands that all selection techniques and devices (including tests) must not discriminate against either sex or any race. All employers, governmental or private, must be able to demonstrate the fairness of their selection procedures. For example:

> Valleyrob Values, a large dressmaking firm, cannot arbitrarily require each new employee to have a high school diploma *unless* the company can demonstrate that all jobs require that much education. Valleyrob can require a certain minimum score on a test; however, it would have to be able to prove, on demand, that this cutoff score discriminates between satisfactory and unsatisfactory employees.

COMPETENCY AND ACCOUNTABILITY

In the previous edition of *Test Scores and What They Mean*, I wrote about still further politicization of testing in the United States. This politicization continues into the present decade. The current emphasis seems to be on student competency and on greater teacher accountability.

An increasing number of states insist that students at all levels be tested to determine their ability to handle academic content suitable to their age and school grade. In many states students are required to pass competency tests as one requirement for high school graduation.

And some states now require that teachers pass tests to show that their knowledge is sufficient to justify their teaching. Teachers have become increasingly accountable to pupils and to their parents for providing quality instruction.

Why has all this occurred? One can speculate that there is greater public impatience because of the frequency of such situations as the following:

> I visited a public high school near my home. Although class was in session, the corridors were so crowded with students that it was difficult to make my way to the principal's office. There were other clusters of students in the men's room, where the smell of cigarette (and marijuana?) smoke struck me immediately upon opening the door.
>
> In another city, a student is stabbed by another student as he leaves the school building. A search of several possible suspects leads to the confiscation of a small arsenal of weapons.
>
> One television sports announcer, as part of his *color* commentary (background information) earlier this season, said: "It's hard to realize that this man was so small when he was in the ninth grade that he was not allowed to play football . . . of course, the ninth grade—that's about the time the school starts teaching cursive." A gross exaggeration, of course, but reflective of the feeling many citizens have of our public schools.

We need, instead, to have more situations such as the following:

> I recently paid an unannounced visit to the high school [Athol (Massachusetts) High School] I had graduated from more than forty years earlier. The principal himself showed me the entire plant of his 900-student school. In every room we visited, there was a cordial exchange between principal and teacher and/or students. The only person we saw in any of the hallways was the head custodian, who had been a classmate of mine. I had one experience that was unique in my visits to schools: the school cafeteria smelled like a place where I would like to eat!

There is a growing belief that schools have been too permissive and that there is a need for a return to more disciplined classrooms—not the old-fashioned *rule of the hickory stick,* but a return to orderly classrooms where students appreciate that a school is a place for learning. The reader may disagree, but I believe that all of this underlies the demands for pupil competence and teacher accountability.

There naturally are problems. A school system must decide how much knowledge and/or skill is required to demonstrate competence. Agencies such as the Educational Testing Service, The Psychological Corporation, and the National Assessment of Educational Progress can assist school systems that wish to develop their own competency tests. It is vitally important that any test used in competency measurement be consistent with the objectives of the particular system that uses it; this applies equally to locally-developed and to standardized tests (as, for example, the National Teacher Examination). Failure to consider local policies (particularly if they are unique in any way) can prove embarrassing—as in the following example taken from industry:

> One company had been using a widely respected test of supervisory practices. Suspicious of seemingly strange results, a personnel worker carefully checked the test items and found disagreement between *right* answers to some items and established company policy.

TEST DISCLOSURE LAWS

At least two states now have laws that require test publishers to disclose full information about the items on tests used as one basis for determining college admission. Similar legislation has been introduced at the federal level, but as of 1985 has not become law.

The intent is commendable: to insure that all examinees have equal information about the purposes of the test, the content areas covered, and the meaning of the score(s). Full disclosure of the items used on the test (together with the scoring key) is quite another matter. The items cannot be used for subsequent testing sessions, for their value has been destroyed. New items must be written and tried out in pilot studies in order to develop new forms of the test. The cost to develop such a new test has been estimated at between $50,000-$165,000; this cost, of course, would have to be passed on to the examinees. The disclosure problem is even more complex if the content domain is limited, for the pool of possible items may soon be exhausted. Ironically, full-disclosure measures may operate in such a way as to defeat the purpose for which they are intended. Research suggests that the brighter and the wealthier students are more likely to benefit most from being able to study the results of previous testings.

PERFORMANCE TESTING

Performance tests are about as old as more verbal tests, but they have rarely been given much attention. The term "performance" is used at least three ways in testing: (1) to refer to the score obtained on any test; (2) to describe a test that requires special apparatus; (3) to describe a job-sample test.

By special apparatus, I mean such items as a formboard (for example, the *Minnesota Spatial Relations Test*) into which pieces must be fitted; a board involving the placement of small blocks or disks (for example, the *Minnesota Rate of Manipulation Test* or the Manual Dexterity Test of the *General Aptitude Test Battery*); or an assembly board (for example, the *Crawford Small Parts Dexterity Test* or the Finger Dexterity Test of the *GATB*). Usually these performance tests are designed to measure finger or hand dexterity, and speed. A slight extension of the term includes block design (as in the Wechsler tests); picture completion (where the examinee tells what part of a picture is missing); or any item that does not involve words in the content of, or in response to, the item.

A job-sample test is one that involves the operation of equipment which one would operate on the job: for example, a power sewing machine, a word processor, or a typewriter. Or it may use a job simulator—especially in situations where the actual equipment is very expensive or potentially hazardous: for example, a flight simulator for pilots or a miniature punch press.

Performance tests are usually expensive, both because of the cost of the apparatus involved and because examinees must ordinarily be tested only one at a time. Efforts to design paper-and-pencil tests as substitutes have not met with great success. There is currently a great deal of research going on, some of it funded in part by the National Institute of Education, to develop new performance tests. Further developments in performance testing are to be expected in the late 1980's.

ADAPTIVE TESTING

Adaptive testing is not new, either. In some respects, even the *Stanford-Binet Scales* are adaptive; so, too, are many teaching-machine programs. Computers seem likely to make adaptive testing commonplace.

In adaptive testing, examinees are presented with one or more items of average difficulty. Examinees who answer correctly are presented with more difficult items; examinees who answer incorrectly are given easier items. This procedure is repeated until examinees are responding to items of difficulty appropriate to determine each person's ability or achievement.

Such testing has obvious advantages. Fewer items are administered to any one examinee, and testing takes less time. A less obvious advantage is the fact that different examinees answer different items—thereby insuring greater security of the pool of available test items.

Other terms synonymous with adaptive testing include: *branched, programmed, staged, selective, tailored, dynamic, individualized,* and *response-contingent.*

COMPUTERS AND TESTING

At one time machine-scoring involved the marking of a special answer sheet that had pairs of parallel lines similar to those shown below. When marked with a number two soft-lead pencil, the answer sheet could be scored by the IBM 805 Test Scoring Machine. The machine could "pick up" and count marks corresponding to the correct responses with electrically-sensitive sensors (the mark-sensing process).

Next came the work of Hankes in Minnesota, Lindquist in Iowa—and the electronics scoring age developed. These machines, in use by major test publishers and several scoring services, depend on *optical scanning* and can operate at very rapid speeds. Some machines are now capable of scoring simultaneously several different tests (or parts of tests) on both sides of answer sheets, reading off student names, preparing rosters, and performing similar operations.

The 1970s saw the development of *electronic-reporting* and *-interpreting* of test results. When computers in line with the scoring machines are fed relevant information, very helpful material can be generated. Several examples follow.

The Psychological Corporation's *Differential Aptitude Tests* may be combined with stated interests and educational-vocational plans to yield a

	A	B	C	D	E
X			∎		
	A	B	C	D	E
Y					∎

computer printout describing the compatibility of these statements with the *DAT* results. Science Research Associates publishes the *Kuder Occupational Interest Survey,* which can be scored only on a computer that correlates the responses made by an examinee with the most common responses made by a group of workers in each of a number of occupations.

The *Strong-Campbell Interest Inventory* is scored only by computer and offers a complex set of scores: 6 themes [based on Holland's theory of vocational choice (Holland, 1973)]; 23 General Interest scores; and 124 Occupational scales. One firm's computerized interpretation averages twenty-four computer printout sheets. Gough's *California Psychological*

Inventory is another test that is often machine-interpreted. One of the most ambitious programs is one developed by Zygmunt A. Piotrowski after years of research, to interpret, by computer, a projective technique, the Rorschach (ink blot) test!

Technology allows examiners to be connected on-line with a scoring service that gives almost instantaneous feedback: scores, interpretation, and a list of specific item responses. The examinee need only sit at a computer terminal and respond to each item as it appears on a monitor. The complete test summary is available in minutes to the examiner.

The widespread use of personal computers offers even greater possibilities. An examiner may have the examinee respond at the computer, as above. Then the examiner can utilize a program designed to score and interpret any number of respected psychological tests. But this very availability of computers and scoring programs promises chaos unless there are better controls. There is fear that the easy availability of programs will lead to indiscriminate use of bootlegged scoring and reporting by unqualified users.

One eminent psychologist has noted that the computer printout of test results is no more a complete psychological assessment than a medical laboratory report is a complete physical examination. It is further noted that no test gains validity through the use of a computer for scoring, and that the value of any interpretation (whether computer-generated or not) depends upon the degree of expertise of the psychologist who prepares it.

The present threat from the use of unlicensed programs by unqualified examiners has prompted a number of test publishers and computer services to organize in an effort to protect both themselves and the legitimate test users. They will include the logo illustrated below in all of their advertising. It is too early to assess how valuable this policy will be. Although some major publishers have subscribed to the practice, there are some others that have not done so. At this writing I am unable to determine whether these latter publishers will eventually join or whether their absence indicates non-agreement with the policy.

LATENT TRAIT SCALING

Latent trait scaling refers to various procedures in the development of test items. These procedures purport to yield items that have common discrim-

inating ability across groups that differ widely in ability. The statistical methodologies are very sophisticated and go well beyond the limits of this book.

Latent trait scaling has found many enthusiastic supporters; however, some psychometricians note that there is little research so far to establish the validity or the utility of the procedures in coping with the challenges of *real* (rather than *theoretical*) data.

If latent trait scaling realizes the promise some believe it has, we may expect to see some marked improvement in tests of the future. Or will it prove to be just another promising, but unrealized, fad? Frankly, I don't know. Further information may be found under the following library listings: *item response theory, item characteristics curve theory,* and *Rasch model.*

3 || THE LANGUAGE OF TESTING

Ms. Schmidt, school counselor, was reporting *interest inventory* results to a high school junior and his father: "John scored high on Computational and Mechanical. This means that he should go on to college and study mechanical engineering."

Maybe John will become a good mechanical engineer. Maybe not. No decision should be made solely on the basis of test scores—and most certainly not just on the results of some interest or preference inventory! What about his intelligence? His aptitudes? His grades in school? His motivation? His willingness to study hard and consistently? His ability to pay for college training? Many factors besides interest-test scores are involved in deciding on any educational or vocational objective.

Interest and aptitude are not synonymous, but some test users do confuse them. There are so many terms used in describing different kinds of tests that it is easy to become confused.

MAXIMUM-PERFORMANCE VERSUS TYPICAL-PERFORMANCE TESTS

All tests may be classified as measuring either *maximum* or *typical performance*. Tests of maximum performance ask examinees to do their best work; ability, either attained or potential, is being tested. With tests of typical performance, we hope to obtain some ideas as to what the examinee is really like or what he actually does, rather than what he is capable of doing.

Maximum-Performance Tests

Maximum-performance tests include tests of intelligence, aptitude, and achievement. In all of these, we assume that all examinees are equally and highly motivated. To the extent that this assumption is not justified, we must discount the results. Since we rarely know how well persons were motivated while taking a test, we usually must accept the assumption or have the person retested.

At least three determinants are involved in every score on a test of maximum performance: innate ability, acquired ability, and motivation. There is no way to determine how much of a person's score is caused by any one of these three determinants—they are all necessarily involved in every maximum-performance score; that is, a person's test score necessarily depends in part on inborn potential as it has been modified by life experiences (education and training, environment, etc.) and by motivation at the time of testing. And, in addition, there is always some error in any measurement. (See reliability.)

Intelligence Tests

Intelligence is an abstract concept. We all have ideas about its meaning, but there is little agreement on its precise meaning. Just as you may have your own definition and I may have my own, so, too, does the author of each intelligence test.

Intelligence tests reflect these differences in definition. Some contain only verbal items; others contain much nonverbal material. Some stress problem-solving while others emphasize memory. Some intelligence tests result in a single total score (probably an IQ) whereas others yield several scores.

These varying emphases lead to diverse results. We should expect to find different IQs when the same person is tested with different tests. We may be obtaining several measures of intelligence, but each time intelligence is being defined just a little differently. Under the circumstances, perhaps we should be surprised whenever different intelligence tests give us nearly the same results.

For most purposes, intelligence tests may be thought of as tests of general aptitude or scholastic aptitude. When so regarded, they are most typically used in predicting achievement in school, college, or training programs. Performance on intelligence tests is related to achievement. Even the ability to take an intelligence test depends on achievement (in reading and arithmetic, for example). And the familiarity with different words, objects, places, and concepts differs from examinee to examinee. Lack of familiarity will put anyone at a disadvantage when taking an intelligence test—one factor that accounts for the lower scores we may find when testing minority youth.

Aptitude Tests

All aptitude tests imply prediction. They give us a basis for predicting future level of performance. Aptitude tests often are used in selecting individuals for jobs, for admission to training programs, for scholarships, and for many other purposes. Sometimes aptitude tests are used for classifying individuals—as when students are assigned to different ability-grouped sections of the same course. Aptitude tests sometimes are substituted for intelligence tests.

The *Differential Aptitude Tests* (*DAT*) and the *Armed Services Vocational Aptitude Battery* (*ASVAB*) are two examples of aptitude test batteries designed to yield scholastic aptitude (or intelligence) scores in addition to the scores on the several aptitude measures. Aptitude measurement depends in part on achievement in such an area as reading.

Achievement Tests

Achievement tests are used in evaluating present level of knowledge, skills, and competence. Unlike other types of tests, many achievement tests are written locally; a teacher's classroom test is a good example. There are also many commercially developed achievement tests. Criterion-referenced tests are further examples of achievement tests. *Assessment* and *evaluation* are terms often used in connection with achievement testing.

The principal basis for differentiating aptitude and achievement tests lies in their use. The same sorts of items—indeed, even the identical test—may be used in different situations to measure aptitude or achievement. The purpose of the testing, whether for assessing present attainment or for predicting future performance, is the best basis for the distinction.

With tests of maximum performance, we seldom have difficulty understanding what we are attempting to measure. With aptitude tests, we are trying to predict how well people will do. With achievement tests, we are trying to measure their present attainment. With intelligence tests, although we may disagree on specific definitions, we are trying to measure the level of intellectual capacity or functioning.

Typical-Performance Tests

The situation is far less clear with typical-performance tests. There is less agreement about what is being measured or what should be measured. To start with, there is such a proliferation of terms: adjustment, personality, temperament, interests, preferences, values; and there are tests, scales,blanks, inventories, indexes, as well as Q-sorts, forced-choice methods, etc.—to say nothing of projective techniques, situational tests, and the like.

What does a score mean? It is very hard to say, even after giving the matter careful thought. In the first place, the dimensions of a typical-performance test are likely to be vaguely defined: what is *sociable* to one author may not be to the next. The philosophy or rationale underlying typical-performance tests must necessarily be more involved and less obvious than the rationale for maximum-performance tests.

Whereas a person's ability is more or less stable, one's affective nature may change over a short period of time. And it is this aspect of the individual that we try to get at through tests of typical performance. We are trying to find out what **Carson is really like** or how **Carrie typically reacts or feels**.

With maximum-performance tests, we are certain at least that people did not obtain higher scores than they are capable of. After all, one cannot fake knowing more algebra or fake being more intelligent. The examinees can, of course, perform far beneath their capabilities—by simply not trying, by paying little attention, or by any of many other means. With typical-performance tests, though, a person usually can fake in either direction (higher or lower, better adjustment or poorer adjustment, etc.). With such tests, we do not want examinees to do the best they can; instead, we want them to answer as honestly as they can. In fact, the purpose of these tests often is disguised. A *Sense of Humor Test* may in reality be an attempt to measure selected dimensions of personality and have little to do with humor.

There would seem to be an assumption that an examinee is trying to answer honestly. Yet on some personality tests the authors have been concerned only with the response made, rather than with the examinee's reasons for having made it. Thus, the person who responds **Yes** to an item may do so honestly, or to look better *or* to look worse than is true; it makes no difference, for a person resembles specified other people at least to the extent of making that same response.

Criterion-Keying

Some typical-performance tests are said to be *criterion-keyed* because their scoring keys have been developed through the performance of two contrasting groups:

> We decide to construct a *Progressivism and Liberalism Index (**PALI**)*. After defining what we mean by progressivism and liberalism, we decide that an ultra-conservative group—say, the James Burke Society (**JBS**)—should obtain very low scores if our test is valid; we decide, too, that members of the American Association for Civil Liberties (**AACL**) should obtain high scores. We write a large number of items that seem relevant and administer them to members of both groups. With the aid of statistics, we retain for our **PALI** those items that discriminate best between the **JBS** and the **AACL**, *regardless* of whether the result seems logical. We might, for example, find more members of **JBS** than members of **AACL** answering **Yes** to: **Do you consider yourself a liberal individual?** Regardless of the real-life accuracy or inaccuracy of the responses, we still might retain this item, counting a response of **No** as one score point in the liberal direction.

Typical-performance tests that are criterion-keyed often seem superior to tests for which the scoring keys have been developed in other ways. Criterion-keyed tests sometimes are criticized because occasional items are scored in a way that seems to make little sense; the answer to this criticism is, of course, that the scoring system "works."

Forced-Choice Items

An item is forced-choice if the alternatives have been matched for social acceptability, but only one alternative relates to a particular criterion. The simplest form of forced-choice item has two alternatives, each seeming to be equally desirable:

> **Would you rather be: (a) honest; (b) loyal?** I would like to be both—and you would, too. Perhaps, though, some group (say, good bookkeepers) could be found statistically to answer **(a)** more often than less good bookkeepers.

Other forced-choice items may involve three or four alternatives, rather than only two. Forced-choice items have the advantage of being somewhat disguised in intent, but they are not unanimously favored. They may be resented by examinees because of the fine discriminations demanded. When used in such a way that the items are scored for more than one variable, they result in an *ipsative* sort of score; that is, the strength of each variable depends not solely on that variable but on its strength relative to the strength of others. In other words, if one variable goes up, another must go down.

Ambiguity of Items

With nearly all typical-performance test items, there is likely to be some ambiguity. Let us look at one item:

I am a liberal.
Strongly Agree   Agree   Uncertain   Disagree   Strongly Disagree

If I had to answer this item, my reasoning might go something like this:

> What do they mean by **liberal**? I could say **Strongly Agree**, for I am strongly opposed to censorship. My political views are moderately conservative, so I could answer **Disagree**. The truth is that sometimes I am liberal and sometimes I am not!

The indecisiveness of an examinee may be caused by the ambiguity of a term, or it may be a reflection of the individual's personality. In either case, the examinee may answer an item sometimes one way and sometimes another and be perfectly sincere each time. (As we shall see later in this chapter, such factors as these lower test reliability.)

Furthermore, the motivational pattern of each examinee becomes of great importance. Examinees who have much to gain by showing up well may try to answer the items so that they appear to be better than they really are, but others may try to appear more disturbed than they really are if that would be to their advantage. Such behaviors may be either deliberate or subconscious.

Still further, most typical-performance tests try to measure several different characteristics of the individual. A person who fakes along one scale of the test may inadvertently change the scores on other measured characteristics as well. For example, the person who tries to appear more *sociable* may inadvertently score lower on the *aggressive* scale.

Often test norms are based on the performances of groups of people (perhaps students) in nonthreatening situations. To compare the performance of a person under stress (such as fear of not being selected or severe personal problems) with the performance of such groups is rather unrealistic.

Typical-performance tests, of course, can be useful to psychologists, experienced counselors, etc.; however, they rarely should be used by people with limited backgrounds in testing and psychology. There are so many pitfalls to be aware of. The tests do have their place—but that place is *not* in the hands of the amateur. Most psychologists believe that somewhat less confidence should be placed in typical-performance tests than in the maximum-performance tests with which this book is principally concerned.

Objective—Subjective—Projective

Another way of looking at tests gives us a classification according to the form of response called for. One familiar classification is *objective* vs. *essay* or better, *objective* vs. *subjective*, and I would add *projective*. A little later

I will mention a similar classification that I prefer even though it is less common.

An item is *objective* if the complete scoring procedure is prescribed in advance of the scoring. Thus multiple-choice and true-false tests are usually objective, for the test writer can draft a scoring key that contains the right (or best) answer for each item on the test. Except for mistakes or for difficulties in reading responses, we can be completely objective. When answered on special answer sheets, such items can be scored by machine. *Subjective* indicates that some element of personal judgment will be involved in the scoring. Completion and essay items are examples of subjective items, for the tester rarely can anticipate every response that may be scored as correct.

I have stressed objectivity of *scoring*. Any time we prepare a test, whether for local use or for national distribution, we must make such decisions as what items to write, what elements of information to include, and what wording to use. Inevitably there is always some degree of subjectivity in test *construction*.

Projective items are, in a sense, subjective items—but they are something more. They are items which are deliberately made ambiguous in order to demand individualistic responses. The Rorschach inkblots and Murray's *Thematic Apperception Test* are examples. Verbal material may be used projectively, too; Rotter, for example, presents the examinee with stems of sentences to be completed, thereby making one *project* his/her personality into the response. Typical of Rotter's items are:

I like to . . .
One thing I dread is . . .
My mother . . .

Select-Response—Supply-Response

A classification that I prefer when looking at test items is *select-response* vs. *supply-response*. This classification, it seems to me, is self-defining: if the examinee may select from among the alternatives given to him, the item is select-response; otherwise, it is a supply-response item. Thus the multiple-choice test is select-response; the essay is supply-response.

Written—Oral—Performance

Another basis for test classification is found in the medium used for presenting the directions and the item material. Most typically, test items are printed or *written*, and the examinee responds by writing answers or by making marks that correspond to chosen answers. Directions sometimes are given orally, but most frequently are given both orally and in writing.

Few tests are *oral*; teacher-prepared spelling tests are the most common example. A few tests are available on sound recordings. There are tests for blind people, some of which were especially developed for them and others that are simply adaptations of tests for the sighted. There are trade tests prepared for oral presentation and oral response, used almost exclusively in employment offices. Nonstandardized oral exams are given in graduate school and other settings. Recently we have seen the development of a few oral aptitude tests for adults who are functionally illiterate.

Performance tests usually involve special apparatus (as opposed to only paper and pencil) and may involve a work sample. See the discussion on page 14.

Standardized—Informal

Standardized tests have been developed, usually by specialists, for more extensive use than by the test-writer and immediate colleagues. The test content is set, the directions prescribed, and the scoring procedure completely specified. And there are norms against which we may compare the scores of our examinees (except on criterion-referenced tests).

Informal tests, on the other hand, refer primarily to tests written by the examiner for local use only. We are not concerned with such tests in this book; however, much that is said about standardized tests does have some application to informal tests, too.

Speed-Power

Speeded tests are maximum-performance tests in which speed plays an important part in determining a person's score; however, a test may have a time limit and still not be speeded. If there is no time limit, or if the time limit is so generous that most examinees are able to finish, the test is said to be a *power* test.

Most achievement tests should be *power* tests, for we are likely to be more concerned with assessing our examinees' levels of attainment than we are in finding out how rapidly they respond. Even here, though, there are exceptions; for example, an achievement test in shorthand or typing.

We have used power and speed as if they were separate categories. It is more accurate to think of them as opposite ends of a continuum. Some tests are almost purely power (having no time limit), and other tests are almost purely speed (having items of such little difficulty that everyone could answer them perfectly if given enough time); but in between these extremes are many tests with time limits, some generous and some limited. Such in-between tests have some characteristics of both speed and power tests and are classified as one or the other depending upon whether time makes speed an important determinant of score.

Group-Individual

This classification is perhaps most obvious of all. An *individual* test is one which can be administered to only one individual at a time. Common examples are individual tests of intelligence, such as the *Stanford-Binet* and the *Wechsler* tests. Some tests that involve special apparatus, such as manual dexterity tests, usually are administered individually; however, such tests sometimes can be administered simultaneously to small groups if proper conditions exist and if the examiner has multiple copies available.

Group tests can be administered to more than one person at a time and usually can be administered simultaneously to a group of any size. Group tests are usually *paper-and-pencil* (the only materials involved), but not necessarily so. Individual tests, however, frequently involve materials other than paper and pencil.

Verbal-Nonverbal

A *verbal* test has verbal items; that is, the items involve words (either oral or written). So-called *nonverbal* tests contain no verbal items; however, words almost always are used in the directions. Some writers prefer the term *nonlanguage* to describe tests that have no verbal items but for which the directions are given either orally or in writing; these writers use *nonverbal* only for tests where no words are used, even in the directions.

Culture-Fair

Some tests are said to be *culture-fair* or *culture-free*. The latter term should be avoided, for no test can be developed completely free from cultural influences. Some tests, though, are relatively independent of cultural or environmental influences and may be thought of as being fair to people of most cultures; however, these tests *may* do less well than others in measuring behavior within our own culture. By using items that are relatively culture-free, tests may not measure any characteristic very effectively within any given culture.

Robert Williams, a well-known black psychologist, has introduced the concept of *cultural homogeneity*—by which he seems to mean simply items that work well within a single culture or subculture. For example, if a black girl does poorly on a standard intelligence test (a test that probably best reflects an upper-middle-class white culture), we might well test her with a black-oriented test (for example, Williams' *BITCH, Black Intelligence Test Culturally Homogeneous*, formerly the *Black Intelligence Test Counterbalanced for Honkies*).

HOW TO TELL

How can we tell what a test is like? We can learn something about available tests by reading the *catalogs* of the various test publishers; however, a test catalog is printed to show the tests a publisher has for sale and is not the most objective source of information.

Nor is the test *title* the best means for telling the purpose of a test. There have been many examples of tests with misleading titles; however, test publishers today tend to do a much better job of giving descriptive titles to their tests [except where they are deliberately disguised (as in some personality tests)].

The test *manual* is usually the best source of detailed information about a test. (See Chapter 5.) This is especially true since 1954 when the American Psychological Association (in cooperation with the American Educational Research Association and the American Personnel and Guidance Association) first published technical recommendations for publishers. Those recommendations were replaced in 1974 with *Standards for Educational and Psychological Tests*; a new edition was published in 1985. Also of great value is a booklet *Principles for the Validation and Use of Personnel Selection Procedures* published in 1975 by APA's Division of Industrial-Organizational Psychology.

The major reference for critical and objective reviews of most psychological tests is provided by the *Mental Measurements Yearbooks*, edited by the late Oscar K. Buros. At this writing there are eight bound issues in the series: the *1938, 1940, Third, Fourth, Fifth, Sixth, Seventh* and *Eighth*; all are needed, for they are essentially nonduplicative. Tests ordinarily are reviewed in subsequent editions only when there is additional evidence to consider. Buros' MMYs are also an excellent source for references to articles about specific tests.

THIS BOOK

Our book is concerned mainly with maximum-performance, objective, select-response, written, standardized group psychometric tests which may be power or speeded and hand- or machine-scored. The book is related primarily to norms-referenced—as opposed to criterion-referenced—measurement.

BASIC ATTRIBUTES OF THE TEST

What test should we use? Is Test B better than Test A? It is important for us all to know at least a little about the characteristics of a good test. At least we should know what to look for when evaluating a test.

Three main attributes will be considered here: *validity*, *reliability*, and *usability*. Validity refers to the ability of the test to do the job we want it to. Reliability means that a test gives dependable or consistent scores. Usability includes all such practical factors as cost, ease of scoring, time required, and the like. These attributes should never be considered as *all* or *none* characteristics, for they are relative to specific situations, uses, groups, etc.

VALIDITY

Validity is the most important single attribute of a good test. Nothing will be gained by testing unless the test has some validity for the use we wish to make of it. A test that has high validity for one purpose may have moderate validity for another, and negligible validity for a third.

> The hypothetical *Mechanical Applications and Practice Test* (**MAP**) has been found highly valid for predicting grades at the Manual Arts High School and for selection of people as machinists' apprentices. It has reasonable, but low, validity for predicting performance in a manual training course and for the selection of people for industrial assembly jobs. The **MAP** is of no value, though, in predicting academic grade-point averages, in selecting industrial sales representatives, or in selecting students to enter engineering colleges. The **MAP**, for some reason that is not immediately apparent, even relates negatively to success in real estate selling; the better sales people tend to score lower on the test.

There are no fixed rules for deciding what is meant by high validity, moderate validity, etc. Skill in making such judgments comes only through training and experience in dealing with tests. The study of a test's validity may be either primarily logical (face or content) or primarily empirical-statistical (criterion-related or construct).

Face Validity

The term *face validity* means simply that the test items look appropriate. Good face validity helps to keep motivation high, for people are likely to try harder when the test seems reasonable. Additionally, good face validity may be important to public relations.

Face validity is the least important indication of validity. Many writers deny that it is validity at all.

Content Validity (Logical Validity)

Somewhat similar, but more systematic and more sophisticated, is *content validity* (otherwise known as *logical validity*, *course validity*, *curricular validity*, or *textbook validity*). Like face validity, content validity is non-statistical; here, however, the test content is examined in detail.

We may check an achievement test to see whether each item covers an important bit of knowledge or involves an important skill related to a particular course or training program. Or we may start off with a detailed outline of our training program and see how thoroughly the test covers its important points.

Content validity is most obviously important in achievement tests, but it can be important with other types. Content validity takes on added importance whenever it is impossible to establish criterion-related validity.

Criterion-Related Validity (Empirical Validity)

Criterion-related validity is implied whenever *validity* is mentioned. This sort of validity is most important in any practical situation. How well does the test measure what we want it to? *Empirical validity* gives us an answer by indicating how closely the test relates to some criterion (that is, to some standard of performance). When empirical validity is high, we can use the test for predicting performance on the criterion variable.

Evidence for this type of validity typically is gained through a validity coefficient, a coefficient of correlation between the test and a criterion.

A correlation coefficient is a statistic that expresses the tendency for values of two variables to change together systematically. It may take any value between 0.00 (no relationship) and +1.00 or −1.00 (each indicating a perfect relationship). Further information on this statistic will be found in Chapter 4.

Factors Influencing Criterion-Related Validity

Skill is required to interpret validity coefficients. In general, the higher the correlation between the test and the criterion, the better; however, other factors have to be considered:

1. Test Variables differ

Some tests lend themselves more naturally to validation studies than do others. For example, school grades are a natural criterion to use in validating a scholastic aptitude test. On the other hand, what would we use as a good criterion for an anxiety scale? Where good criteria are hard to find, we usually cannot expect high validity coefficients; sometimes, in fact, the test may be a better measure of the characteristic than any criterion is. For example: a standardized achievement test is usually superior to a teacher-made classroom achievement test.

2. Criteria differ

The criterion used in one validation study may be more important or more relevant to our purposes than the criterion used in other validation studies.

We want a test to help us in the selection of bookbinders. *The Health Analysis Form* correlates 0.65 with record of attendance; the *Hand Dexterity Test* correlates 0.30 with number of books bound during an observation period. Which test should we use? Should we use both? We would need more information, of course, but we would certainly want to consider which criterion (attendance record or production record) is more important to know.

3.   Groups differ

For any number of reasons, the test that works well with one group may not do so with another group. The test that discriminates between bright and dull primary school pupils may be worthless when used with high school students because all high school students get near-perfect scores. Consider also the following:

> The *Aytown Advertiser* finds that the *Typographers Own Performance Scale (TOPS)* is very helpful in selecting good printers and in reducing turnover among printers, but that it is no good in selecting reporters and office workers. *The Beetown Bugle* finds that the *TOPS* is of little value in selecting its printers. (This is entirely possible, for the two newspapers may have different standards of quality, the labor markets may differ in the two cities, etc.)

4.   Variability differs

Validity coefficients are likely to be higher when the group of examinees shows a wide range of scores. A casual glance may tell us that John (a basketball center) is taller than Bill (who is of average height), but it may take a close look to tell whether Bill is taller than Tom (who is also of average height). In much the same way, a crude test can discriminate well if there are gross differences among those tested, but a much better test may not discriminate adequately if the group is highly homogeneous.

> At a conservatory of music, I once found that the best predictor of grades was a (not very good) intelligence test—not any measure of musical knowledge or judgment of musical ability. On these latter measures, the range (a variability statistic) was restricted—all applicants being well above general population averages; however, there was much greater variability of scores on the intelligence test.

5.   Practical factors

With today's emphasis on fairness in testing, the examiner may wish to determine empirical validity separately for different groups. The test that has high validity for one sex or for one race may not have comparable validity for the other sex or for another race; however, such differences are less common than generally supposed.

6.   Additional information

A validity coefficient must also be evaluated in terms of how much additional information it will give us. One test may correlate very high with a criterion variable, but still not help us much. This situation is likely to occur whenever the test also correlates very high with information we already have (for example, scores from another test or previous school grades). In other words, the test will not be helpful unless it contributes something *new* to understanding the examinees; this increase is sometimes called *incremental validity*. (Note: If this were not so, we could give several different forms of a valid test to each examinee and, eventually, get perfect validity. In reality, we can get only a slight increase in validity in this manner.)

These six considerations are only illustrative of why we cannot assert flatly, "the higher the validity coefficient, the better." Other things being equal, the statement will be true; however, we must be sure that other things *are* equal.

Criterion-related validity may be either *concurrent* or *predictive*. Sometimes these have been treated as separate types of validity, but they are better described as both being instances of empirical validity, for they differ only in time sequence. In concurrent validity, both test scores and criterion values are obtained at about the same time. In predictive validity, there is some lapse in time between testing and obtaining the criterion values.

Construct Validity

With *construct validity*, there is no obvious criterion. There may be no natural criterion, for example, for an anxiety scale; however, we may be able to identify several groups of people who would seem to be more anxious (according to the test's definition of anxiety). Such groups might include students who ask questions of a teacher the day before a test, students who visit the campus counseling service, etc. A study showing such people having higher scores than others in a control group would be some evidence of the test's criterion validity.

Construct validity involves an effort to understand the psychological meaningfulness of both the test and the rationale that lies behind the test. Increasingly the term is coming to refer to the entire body of accumulated research on a test.

The topic of construct validity is a complex one. Further details may be obtained from any psychological or educational measurement textbook.

RELIABILITY

Test reliability is very important to the test user, for it is necessary (but not sufficient) for good validity; that is, a test can be highly reliable without necessarily being valid for any purpose of interest to us.

A classroom teacher would have little confidence in the standardized achieve-ment test in mathematics that placed Laura in the top 10% of her class last month but places her at about the median today. The industrial personnel person would care little for the selection test which ranked Travis Taylor in the bottom quarter of the applicants' norms group a few weeks ago but ranks him in the top quarter of the same group today.

Reliability refers to the *reproduce-ability* of a set of test results. A test with high reliability is one that will yield very much the same relative scores for a group of people under differing conditions or situations.

Note that it is the *relative size* of score—not necessarily the exact same scores. If everyone's scores were to change by the same (or proportional) amount under the two conditions, the reliability would still be perfect.

Any factor that tends to exert a varying or changeable influence on a set of test scores has an adverse effect on the reliability of the test. We say that such factors contribute to the *error variance* of the test.

We can never tell exactly how much error variance is present in a set of scores. We can, however, estimate how much error variance there is. And that is essentially what we do when we compute reliability coefficients (i.e., correlation coefficients between two versions of the test scores of the same group of individuals). There are different types of reliability coeffi-cients, each of which tells us something—but not everything—about the reliability of the test scores.

When we read test manuals, we need to look carefully at the reliability coefficients reported. We can sometimes get a good estimate of how stable and consistent we may expect results from a test to be. There are some sources of error variance, however, which are not included in any of the common estimates of reliability. On the other hand, all sources of error operate to keep any *validity* coefficient from being unrealistically high.

Lyman's Five Dimensions of Reliability

What are some of the sources of error variance? We can consider them reasonably well using a five-dimensional model; that is, by consider-ing five different influences. But remember that *anything* which affects scores differentially increases the amount of error variance and lowers the reliability and (indirectly) the validity.

1. Examinee-incurred

Some error variance is contributed more by the individual examinee than by anything else. For example: the motivation of the examinee at the times tested—to the extent that motivation varies, the resulting test scores vary and will be unreliable. But the individuals may also vary in other significant ways: in physical health, mental alertness, stamina, competitive spirit, willingness to ask questions when directions are incompletely understood, ability to follow directions, or efficiency of work habits. These are just suggestive of the near-infinite ways the examinees themselves may introduce variable influences that will tend to lower measured test reliability.

None of the common methods of estimating test reliability gets at any of these examinee-incurred influences; however, we try to minimize these influences whenever we have charge of a testing session—by trying to insure that all individuals are ready, willing, and desirous of doing their best on the test. We cannot completely eliminate this type of error variance. We can try to keep it minimal.

2. *Examiner-scorer influence*

This source of error variance can be, and often is, negligible. Variable errors attributable to the examiner and scorer of most standardized paper-and-pencil tests are seldom of great magnitude; however, they can be. In their efforts to have their students do as well as they can on a standardized achievement test or an intelligence test, teachers sometimes invalidate the test by giving extra help, pointing out mistakes, or allowing additional time. An overly strict, rigid, or angry examiner may reduce the test's reliability, for this non-standard behavior will be reacted to differentially by the various examinees. Examiner influences have the most adverse effects on the scores of young and inexperienced examinees. Relatively mature, test-wise examinees who are well-motivated can tolerate a great deal without being badly affected. Typically, persons who administer a standardized paper-and-pencil test contribute little to error variance if they follow test directions.

The examiner is likely to be a major source of error variance on individual tests (for example, the *Stanford-Binet*, the *Wechsler* tests, the *Rorschach*, etc.)

The literature is full of research showing that there can be large differences in the test results obtained by different examiners; and this, of course, is just another way of saying that error variance may be relatively great in a set of results from such tests.

But notice that we have also included the *scorer* element here. If the test can be scored objectively, there can be perfect scorer reliability. Only when there is an element of subjectivity in the grading of tests does scorer reliability become a factor—as, for example, in the scoring of individual tests of intelligence and of personality. Where there is subjectivity of scoring, the test manual should mention scorer reliability. Errors in recording or in copying results may be further sources of error.

3. *Test content*

Some of the most common reliability coefficients are those relating to test content. A test, being merely a sample of the items that might have been written from the same content domain, offers a major source of error variance. The scores obtained by a group of examinees might have differed a great deal if different questions had been asked. When there are alternate forms of a test, we can obtain an estimate of content reliability by administering both forms to the same group of people and determining the correlation between the two sets of scores.

Provided the test is not highly speeded, evidence of the content reliability may be obtained from one administration of a single form of a test. One common way of doing this is through the use of an internal consistency measure such as one of the Kuder-Richardson formulas. These formulas involve assumptions about the test items and total score, but these assumptions are reasonable to make about many tests.

Also common with non-speeded tests is the split-half (sometimes called odd-even) reliability coefficient.

> We score each person's paper twice: once for the odd-numbered items only and once for the even-numbered items only. We find the correlation between the odd-item and even-item scores; however, this correlation coefficient is an underestimate of the test's reliability, for longer tests tend to be more reliable than shorter ones—and we have correlated two half-length tests; however, we can estimate the full-length test's reliability from a formula (known as the *Spearman-Brown prophecy formula*).

4. Time influence

The fourth type of contribution to error variance is probably the best known of all: time influences. *Temporal reliability* is estimated by giving the same test to the same group at two different times, and by correlating scores made on the first and second administrations of the test. *Coefficients of stability* are almost always reported in test manuals and are reasonably well understood by most test users.

If the second administration is given very shortly after the first, some people may remember specific items—and this will influence the results. With some kinds of tests, the difficulty level of the items is changed considerably once a person has taken the test; as, for example, when much of the difficulty depends on having the examinee determine how to solve some type of problem. If the time interval between testings is very long, real changes may have taken place in the examinees and test scores should be different; in such situations, the ability of the test to reflect these real changes in the people will result in a spuriously low reliability coefficient because the changes in score are not the fault of the test. For example:

> Fourth-grade pupils are tested at the beginning and retested at the end of the school year; all pupils will have learned something, but some will have learned much more than others. Inexperienced machinists, retested after six months on the job, will show the same sort of pattern—some people having changed

appreciably, some having changed little. People undergoing psychotherapy between first and second testings may show markedly different scores.

5. *Situation-induced*

By the test *situation*, I am referring to those aspects of the total testing picture that are not clearly attributable elsewhere.

At a testing conference years ago, one participant asked: "What is the effect on test reliability of a sudden, preseason, unexpected blizzard?" Would there be any effect on the test scores of a class of children being tested under such a condition? Certainly there would be, but it would be impossible to estimate just how much. Little Alicia Alvarez may be worried that her mother won't be able to get to the school to pick her up. Freckle-faced Timmy Tolpin may be stimulated to do his very best work as he looks forward to some after-school sledding. But Timmy's steady-minded sister, Rosie, probably would do just about the same as she would have done under normal weather conditions.

Testing conditions can make a great deal of difference in test results. Such conditions as: ventilation, noise level, sound distractions, lighting, overcrowding, writing surface, and the like—all *can* (but usually don't) have a major adverse effect on reliability.

> Take "writing surface" for example. Suppose a highly speeded test is being taken by a group of high school students or by a group of job applicants. Suppose further that some examinees have those pencil-rutted, hand-carved desktops; some have to take the test while balancing lapboards; and some have good, roomy, smooth desk tops on which to take their tests. Is there any question as to whether some of the examinees will be unable to do their best work? The writing surface will contribute considerable error variance in this situation.

Cheating is another variable error. The examinee is helped by an indeterminate amount (perhaps even by a negative amount) by his cheating.

These influences, although potentially important, are hard to estimate—and do not enter into any of the common reliability coefficients. Most of these testing-condition influences are subject to control by the examiners if they plan carefully in advance of the testing session. In all fairness, too, most situational influences can be overcome by reasonably experienced and highly motivated examinees. They produce more unreliability with younger, less experienced, and less confident examinees.

Interrelationship of Sources of Error Variance

Some reliability coefficients take several sources of error variance into consideration. For example, some test manuals report test-retest reliability coefficients with alternate forms of the test being used—clearly taking cognizance of both content and temporal influences. In general, test publishers do a good job of reporting on content and temporal influences but do less well on the others.

Standard Error of Measurement

The reliability of test scores may also be expressed in terms of the standard error of measurement. This standard error tells us how much one's obtained score is likely to differ from the examinee's hypothetical true score. This concept is explained further on page 55.

Factors Affecting Reliability

Thousands of pages have been written on test reliability; we will do little more here than suggest a few of the factors which influence reliability.

1. Length increases reliability

The longer the test, the more reliable it will be—provided other factors are held constant (for example, the group tested is the same, the new items are as good as those on the shorter test, and the test does not become so long that fatigue is a consideration).

2. Heterogeneity increases reliability

The variability of the group tested is also important in evaluating any reliability coefficient. If everything else is the same, higher reliability coefficients will be found for groups which vary more in ability.

We are going to demonstrate the temporal reliability of a *Reading Speed Test* *(RST)*. From our school system we select at random one pupil from each grade, one through nine. We test each child in this sample; one week later, we test them all again. Inasmuch as speed of reading increases through these grades, we should have a tremendous range in scores—and the differences among pupils should be so great that order of score is not likely to change from one administration of the test to the next. The reliability coefficient then would prove to be very high. If, on the other hand, we were to select a small group of average-ability second-graders and test them twice (as above) on the *RST*, we should find a lower reliability *coefficient*; these pupils probably would not differ much in their initial scores—and order of score might very well change on the second testing, thereby reducing the size of the reliability *coefficient*. (This latter example is appropriate; the former is not.)

We need to study carefully the publisher's description of the group used and the conditions of testing in any reliability report.

3. Shorter time, higher reliability

The length of time between the two testings in a temporal reliability coefficient is of obvious importance. Reliability is higher when the time between the two testings is short. That is one reason why IQs change most when there is a long period of time between testings.

4. Type of reliability estimate

Reliability coefficients will differ according to the type of reliability estimate being used.

Comparing Validity and Reliability

Validity is established through a statistical comparison of scores with values on some outside variable. Any constant error in the test will have a direct adverse effect on the test's validity.

> We want to select power sewing machine operators. We use a test which contains many difficult words that are not related to sewing machine operation. Since this extraneous factor will influence each individual's score in a consistent fashion, the difficult words will reduce the test's validity for our purpose. (Note that the reliability is not necessarily reduced.)

No outside variable is involved in reliability, for reliability is not concerned with *what* a test measures—only with its reproduce-ability of test results. Irregularities in testing procedures have a direct and adverse effect on reliability; indirectly, they may reduce validity as well. (These are *variable* errors. Variable here simply means nonconstant. In most other places throughout this book, *variable* is a general term referring to any characteristic, test, or the like which may assume different values.) The size of a validity coefficient is limited mathematically by the size of the reliability coefficient.

USABILITY

The third basic attribute of a test is *usability*. This includes all the many practical factors that go into our decision to use a particular test.

> We are wondering whether to use the *Lyman Latin Verb Test (LLVT)* or the *Latin Original Verb Examination (LOVE)* in our high school Latin course. Since both tests are hypothetical, we may give them any characteristics we desire. My *LLVT*, therefore, has perfect reliability and validity. The *LOVE*, although not perfect, does have respectable validity and reliability for our purposes. We'll probably decide to use the *LOVE* in spite of the *LLVT*'s perfection, for the *LLVT* takes two weeks to administer and an additional week to score, can be administered to only to one examinee at a time, costs $8,000 per examinee, and only one person is considered qualified to administer and score it. The *LOVE*, on the other hand, can be given to a group of students simultaneously, has reusable test booklets which cost only eighty cents per copy (answer sheets cost ten cents apiece), and can be scored by a clerical worker in two or three minutes.

Under usability, we deal with all sorts of practical considerations. A longer test may be more reliable, even more valid; however, if we have only a limited time for testing, we may have to compromise with that ideal. If the preferred test is too expensive, we may have to buy a different one instead (or buy fewer copies of the first test), and so on.

I am not suggesting that validity and reliability are important only in theory. They are vitally important. There is no point in testing unless we can have some confidence in the results. Practical factors must be considered, but *only* if the test has satisfactory reliability and validity.

4 A FEW STATISTICS

Lots of people are either bored by, or frightened of, statistics. What a pity! Statistics is a study with a lurid past, a fascinating present, and a limitless future. But more important for us right here is the fact that basic statistics are easy to understand—you should have no difficulty with this chapter if you've completed eighth-grade mathematics.

INTRODUCTION

Fifty people who applied for jobs at the Culinary Crafts Company took the *Cooking Arts Test*. They obtained the following scores (where one point was given for each correct answer):

AA	65	AK	33	AU	35	BE	43	BO	34
AB	40	AL	50	AV	54	BF	43	BP	49
AC	55	AM	26	AW	44	BG	35	BQ	30
AD	49	AN	54	AX	50	BH	54	BR	38
AE	24	AO	42	AY	45	BI	44	BS	62
AF	48	AP	26	AZ	44	BJ	52	BT	42
AG	56	AQ	47	BA	41	BK	47	BU	48
AH	37	AR	31	BB	48	BL	50	BV	61
AI	50	AS	47	BC	62	BM	31	BW	50
AJ	29	AT	51	BD	43	BN	38	BX	46

Frequency Distribution

To visualize those *CAT* scores better, we might put them into a *frequency distribution*—an orderly arrangement, usually from highest to lowest, showing the frequency with which each score occurs—as in Table 4.1:

TABLE 4.1* **Scores Made By 50 Job Applicants At The Culinary Crafts Company On The Cooking Arts Test**

SCORE	TALLIES	*f*	SCORE	TALLIES	*f*	SCORE	TALLIES	*f*	SCORE	TALLIES	*f*
65	|	1	55	|	1	45	|	1	35	||	2
64		0	54	|||	3	44	|||	3	34	|	1
63		0	53		0	43	|||	3	33	|	1
62	||	2	52	|	1	42	||	2	32		0
61	|	1	51	|	1	41	|	1	31	||	2
60		0	50	⸝⸝⸝⸝	5	40	|	1	30	|	1
59		0	49	||	2	39		0	29	|	1
58		0	48	|||	3	38	||	2	28		0
57		0	47	|||	3	37	|	1	27		0
56	|	1	46	|	1	36		0	26	||	2
									25		0
									24	|	1

*Hypothetical data

Often we can get an even better idea of the scores if we arrange them into *class intervals*; that is, the units (usually greater than one) used in a frequency distribution. The use of class intervals gives us a method for grouping together several adjacent score values—to enable us to (1) graph the distribution meaningfully, and (2) compute certain statistics more easily.

We aim for approximately 15 intervals (a good compromise between too few and too many) to span the range of scores. We try to have each interval an odd-numbered width, so that each *midpoint* will be an integer (whole number).

For these data: *Range* = 65 − 24 = 41; 41 ÷ 15 is approximately 3 (an odd number). Thus, we select 64-66 as the interval 3 units in width to contain score values of 64, 65, and 66. [Since we are treating these scores as continuous (see below), the *real* limits of the interval are 63.5 and 66.5; checking, we find that those values are 3 units apart, 66.5 − 63.5 = 3.] The frequency distribution has now become as shown in Table 4.2.

Continuous values are the results of measuring, rather than counting. We cannot have absolute accuracy, for we might always use still finer instruments to obtain greater precision. We can measure relatively tangible variables such as length and weight with considerable accuracy but find it harder to measure accurately such intangibles as intelligence, attitude, and neuroticism. The principle is the same: absolute precision of measurement

TABLE 4.2   Use Of Class Intervals (Of 3 Units Each) For Data In Table 4.1

CLASS INTERVAL	f	CLASS INTERVAL	f	CLASS INTERVAL	f
64-66	1	49-51	8	34-36	3
61-63	3	46-48	7	31-33	3
58-60	0	43-45	7	28-30	2
55-57	2	40-42	4	25-27	2
52-54	4	37-39	3	22-24	1

is not possible with any variable. The degree of accuracy depends on the nature of the variable itself, the precision of the instrument, and the nature of the situation.

> See how this works with *length*. In discussing the size of my office, I may use dimensions accurate to the nearest foot. I may note my desk size to the nearest inch. I measure the height of my grandchildren to the nearest quarter-inch. My model-builder friends do work that is accurate to the nearest one one-hundredth inch. And scientists working on our space program need even greater precision.

Some variables can be expressed only as *discrete values*. Here we count, and complete accuracy is possible: number of volumes in the public libraries of Ohio, number of students in each room at Aiken High School, number of seats in each Cincinnati theater, and so on. The tipoff is the phrase *number of*. When the variable is expressed that way, we usually have a discrete variable.

If we think of a test as a collection of questions and of test scores as the number of items correct, we have to consider test scores as discrete values. We do often obtain scores by counting the number of correct answers; however, we usually want to consider the test scores as measures of some characteristic beyond the test itself.

We are not satisfied with thinking of AA merely as having answered correctly sixty-five items on the *CAT*. Rather, we want to consider this 65 as indicating some amount of the ability that underlies the test.

Any test is a mere sample of the items that might have been included. We hope that the test is a representative sample of this universe (or population or domain) of all possible items. The universe of possible items for most tests is almost infinite, for we could not possibly write all the items which would be relevant. We find it helpful to think of any psychological or educational test as being a rather crude instrument for *measuring* whatever characteristic (ability, knowledge, aptitude, interest, and so on) is presumed to underlie the test. Although not everyone agrees, most test authorities treat test scores as *continuous*, and we shall do so in this book.

The Histogram

We may show those *CAT* results graphically by marking off all possible score values (within the range of scores obtained) along a horizontal line. This horizontal line, called the *abscissa*, serves as the baseline of our graph. If we use a tiny square to represent each applicant, we will have a graph like that shown in Figure 4.1.

Since the scores are continuous, we let each of those little squares occupy the space of one full unit (or class interval); each square occupies a space from the *real lower* limit to the *real upper* limit. AA's score was 65, and the square is placed so that it extends to the real limits of the interval, thereby having half of its area above and half below the *midpoint* of the interval (65.0).

We can tell the number of cases (the frequency) in any interval by counting the number of squares above it or, even more simply, by reading the number on the ordinate (the vertical axis) of the graph at a height level with the top of the column. This type of graph is called a *histogram*.

When we draw a graph to show a set of scores, we ordinarily make no effort to retain the identity of the individuals. We are less interested in knowing AA's score or AB's score than we are in portraying the general nature of the scores made by the group. We are interested in general characteristics such as the shape of the distribution, the scores obtained most frequently, and the range in scores. Ordinarily, therefore, we would be more likely to draw the histogram in one of the ways shown in Figure 4.2.

Here we have no need for individual squares; instead, we draw columns (each the same width) to the height required to show appropriate frequency.

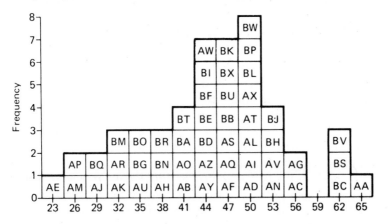

FIGURE 4.1. Raw Score Values on the Cooking Arts Test.

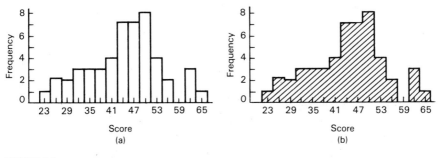

FIGURE 4.2.

Frequency Polygon

Another type of graph that may be used for the same purpose is the frequency polygon. A dot is placed above the midpoint of each score value (or each class interval) at a height corresponding to the number of people making that score. Each of these dots is connected with the two adjacent dots by straight lines. In addition, the distribution is extended one unit (that is, either one score value or one class interval) beyond the highest and lowest scores obtained. This means that there will be lines to the baseline at each extreme, thereby completing the figure and making our graph a polygon (a many-sided figure).

Figure 4.3 is a frequency polygon showing the test scores of the fifty Culinary Crafts Company applicants; we have used class intervals that are three score values wide and show the same information displayed in Figures 4.1 and 4.2.

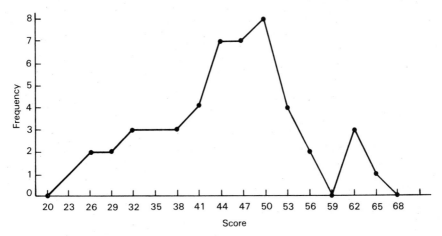

FIGURE 4.3.

It can be shown mathematically that a histogram and a frequency polygon showing the same data and drawn to the same scale are identical in area. This is important, for it is *area* that is proportional to frequency of cases.

DESCRIPTIVE STATISTICS

After a little practice, we can learn a great deal from a graph; however, descriptive statistics provide a more precise means for summarizing or describing a set of scores. Descriptive statistics includes measures of position (including central tendency), measures of variability, and measures of covariability.

Measures of Position (Other than Central Tendency)

Measures of position are numbers which tell us where a specified person or a particular score value stands within a set of scores. In a graph, any measure of position is located as a *point* on the baseline.

1. Rank

Rank is the simplest description of position—first for the best (or highest), second for the next best, third, etc., on to the last. Its assets are its familiarity and its simplicity; however, its interpretation is so dependent on the size of the group that it is actually less useful than one might think. We never use it formally in describing test results.

2. Percentile rank

Percentile Rank is a better position indicator because it makes allowance for difference in the size of the group. Percentile rank is a statement of a person's relative position within a defined group—thus a percentile rank of 30 indicates a score that is as high as or higher than those made by 30 percent of the people in that particular group. Percentile ranks are widely used as a type of test score and will be considered in detail in Chapter 6.

Measures of Central Tendency (Averages)

A measure of *central tendency* is designed to give us a single value that is most characteristic or typical of a set of scores. Three such measures are fairly common in testing: the mean, the median, and the mode. Each of these may be located as a *point* along the abscissa of a graph.

1. Mean

The most common measure of position and of central tendency is the *arithmetic mean* (usually called simply the *mean*). This is nothing more than the average we learned in elementary school. But *average* is a generic term and may refer to any measure of central tendency. The mean is the preferred measure for general use with test scores. Besides certain mathematical advantages, the mean is widely understood and easy to compute. We use the mean unless there is good reason to prefer some other statistic.

In grade school we learned to find the mean by adding up all the scores and dividing by the number of scores. Stated as a formula, this becomes

$$\overline{X} = \frac{\Sigma X}{N}$$

where $\overline{X}$ = the mean of Test X
Σ = "add the values of"
X = raw score on Test X
N = number of cases (number of persons for whom we have scores)

2. Median

With income data, we are likely to have one very high salary (or, at best, a very few high salaries) and many more lower salaries. The result is that the mean tends to exaggerate the salaries (i.e., it is pulled toward the extreme values), and the median becomes the preferred measure. The *median* is that value above which fall 50 percent of the cases and below which fall 50 percent of the cases; thus it is less likely to be drawn in the direction of the extreme cases.

Income data are usually positively skewed, having many low values and a few high values. This same shape of distribution, shown in Figure 4.4(a), is frequently found when a test is difficult or when the examinees are not well prepared. Figure 4.4(b) is negatively skewed, the sort of distribution we are likely to get when a test is too easy for the group tested. The mean gives us an erroneous impression of central tendency whenever a distribution is badly skewed, and the median becomes the preferred measure.

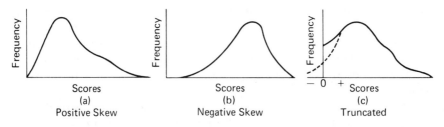

FIGURE 4.4. Three Nonsymmetrical Distributions.

The median is also preferred when a distribution is truncated (cut off in some way so that there can be no cases beyond a certain point). In Figure 4.4(c) the distribution is truncated, perhaps because of a very difficult test on which zero was the lowest score assigned; the dotted line suggests the distribution we might have obtained if the scoring had permitted the assignment of negative scores.

Since the median is the fiftieth percentile (also the second quartile and the fifth decile), it is the logical measure of central tendency to use when percentile ranks are being used. For computation, see percentiles (pages 92-96).

3. Mode

The third type of average used with test scores is the *mode*. The mode is the most commonly obtained score or the midpoint of the score interval having the highest frequency.

The mode is rarely usable in connection with further computations. It is very easily found, however, and we can use it as a quick (and rough) indication of central tendency. If the scores are arranged in a frequency distribution, the mode is equal to the midpoint of the score (or class interval) which has the highest frequency. If a distribution of scores is graphed, the mode is even more quickly found—it will be the value (on the baseline) at the point above which the curve is at its highest point, as shown in Figure 4.5. Sometimes there are two modes (bimodal) or even more modes (multimodal) to a distribution. Graphs (c) and (d) in Figure 4.5 are both bimodal even though the peaks in (d) are not exactly of equal height.

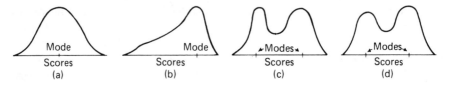

FIGURE 4.5. The Mode.

Comparison of the Central Tendency Measures

Let's review briefly. The mean is the best measure of central tendency in most testing situations. We use it unless there is some good reason not to. It is widely understood and fairly easily computed. It fits logically and mathematically into the computation of other statistics. On the other hand, the mean should not be used when the distribution of scores is *badly* skewed or truncated, because it is not a good indicator of central tendency in such situations.

The median fits logically into the percentile scale. Its use is preferred whenever distributions are truncated or badly skewed. It involves fewer

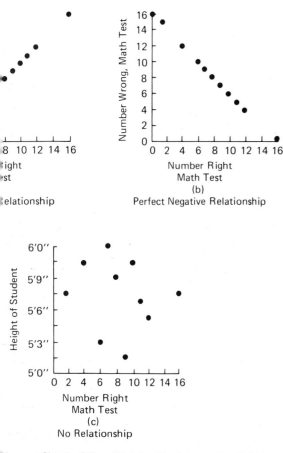

Number Wrong, Math Test

Number Right
Math Test
(b)
Perfect Negative Relationship

Height of Student

Number Right
Math Test
(c)
No Relationship

Diagrams Showing Different Relationships Between Two Variables.

o regular order to the dots in Figure 4.6(c), for this is a
ficient of 0.00—no correlation at all, neither positive nor
again, the Number Right is shown along the abscissa, but
e shown Height of Student along the ordinate. Apparently,
ency for math scores and heights to be related.

encounter a perfect correlation in actual practice. Only
kely to encounter any correlation coefficients above 0.90
ility coefficients (see "Reliability" in Chapter 3). Validity
"Validity" in Chapter 3) are much more likely to run
.20 and 0.60 depending upon the test, the criterion, and
scores within the group tested.

shows a correlation coefficient of approximately 0.50. This
atter diagram we might reasonably expect to find for the
een a test and its criterion; in fact, such a correlation may
good validity coefficient. Note, however, that we would not

mathematical assumptions than the mean. Although less widely used than the mean, it is easily understood and easily computed.

The mode is less widely used than either the mean or the median. It provides a quick and easy estimate of central tendency, but it is not especially useful in connection with test scores.

There are still other measures of central tendency, but none is commonly used in testing. Any measure of central tendency can be located as a *point* along the abscissa of a graph.

Measures of Variability

It is possible for two distributions of scores to have a similar (even identical) central tendency value and yet be very different. The scores in one distribution, for example, may be spread over a far greater range of values than those in the other distribution. These statistics tell us how much variability (or dispersion) there is in a distribution; that is, they tell us how scattered the scores are. In graphic work, each variability measure is shown as a *distance* along the baseline.

1. Range

The *range* is familiar to all of us, representing the difference between the highest and lowest scores. The range is easily found and easily understood, but is valuable only as a rough indication of variability. It is the least stable measure of variability, depending entirely on the two most extreme (and, therefore, least typical) scores. It is less useful in connection with other statistics than other measures of variability.

2. Semi-interquartile range

This statistic defines itself: *semi* (half) *inter* (between) *quartile* (one of three points dividing the distribution into four groups of equal size) *range* (difference or distance). The statistic equals one-half the distance between the extreme quartiles, Q_3 (seventy-fifth percentile) and Q_1 (twenty-fifth percentile).

We use the semi-interquartile range (or quartile deviation) as a measure of dispersion whenever we use the median as the measure of central tendency. It is preferred to other measures when a distribution of scores is truncated or badly skewed. The formula for the semi-interquartile range is:

$$Q = \frac{Q_3 - Q_1}{2}$$

where Q = semi-interquartile range
Q_3 = third quartile, the seventy-fifth percentile (P_{75})
Q_1 = first quartile, the twenty-fifth percentile (P_{25})

3. *Average deviation (mean deviation)*

Another statistic which has been used to express variability is the average deviation or mean deviation. Its chief advantage is the simplicity of its rationale, for it is simply the mean *absolute* amount by which scores differ from the mean score; however, it is seldom used today. It is mentioned *only* because there are occasional references to it in testing literature.

4. *The standard deviation*

Although its rationale is less obvious than in other measures of variability, the *standard deviation* is the best such measure. It is the most dependable measure of variability, for it varies less than other measures from one sample to the next. It fits mathematically with other statistics. It is widely accepted as the best measure of variability and is of special value to test users because it is the basis for (1) standard scores; (2) a way of expressing the reliability of a test score; (3) a way of indicating the accuracy of values predicted from a correlation coefficient; and (4) a common statistical test of significance. This statistic, in short, is one which *every test user should know thoroughly*.

The standard deviation is equal to the square root of the mean of the squared deviations from the distribution's mean. Although more efficient computational formulas exist for the standard deviation, the following formula is descriptive:

$$s_x = \sqrt{\frac{\Sigma\,(X - \overline{X})^2}{N}}$$

where
s_x = standard deviation of Test X
$\sqrt{}$ = "take the square root of"
Σ = "add the values of"
X = raw score on Test X
$\overline{X}$ = mean of Test X
N = number of persons whose scores are involved

What does the standard deviation mean? As a measure of variability it can be expressed as a distance along the baseline of a graph. The standard deviation is often used as a unit in expressing the difference between two specified score values; differences expressed in this fashion are more comparable from one distribution to another than they would be if expressed as raw scores.

The standard deviation is also frequently used in making interpretations from the normal curve (described later in this chapter). In a normal distribution, 34.13 percent of the area under the curve lies between the mean and a point that is one standard deviation away from it; 68.26 percent of the area lies between a point that is one standard deviation below the mean and a point one standard deviation above the mean. In nonnor-

mal distributions (and perfect nor[...] figure will not be exactly 68.26 p[...] percentage. In other words, appro[...] thirds of the cases, for area repres[...] one standard deviation of the me[...] one-third of the cases will be more [...] the mean.

5. *Probable error (PE)*

The probable error is rarel[...] quently in older testing literature.[...] deviation by the constant value, [...] when few people understood eve[...] determine the points ($\pm$ 1 *PE* [...] percent of the cases and beyond [...] *normal distribution.*

The probable error has only [...] combine with other measures—a[...] standard deviation must be comp[...]

Measures of Covariability

Measures of *covariability* tell [...] two tests (or other variables). The [...] ods, but we shall consider only t[...] moment correlation coefficient an[...] tion coefficient.

Correlation is the degree [...] cialized techniques, even more) [...] index number expressing the deg[...] from 0.00 (no relationship) to [...] $-$ 1.00 (perfect negative correl[...] impractical) examples to illustrate[...]

In Figure 4.6(a) we see a p[...] have taken a math test. Their scor[...] abscissa and as Percent Right alo[...] diagram represents one student's [...] and Percent Right. Since there is [...] straight line. Since the correlatior[...] left to upper right.

In Figure 4.6(b) we see a pe[...] the same ten students with their [...] abscissa) and Number Wrong (al[...] straight line, but proceed from u[...] of negative correlations.

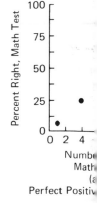

FIGURE 4.6.   Scatt[...]

There is[...] correlation co[...] negative. Onc[...] this time we h[...] there is no te[...]

We neve[...] rarely are we [...] except as reli[...] coefficients (s[...] between abou[...] the variability[...]

Figure 4.[...] is the sort of [...] correlation be[...] be a reasonabl[...]

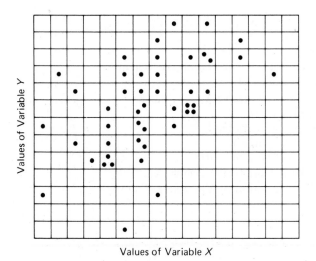

Values of Variable *X*

FIGURE 4.7. Scatter Diagram Showing Correlation Coefficient of Approximately 0.50 Between Variable *X* and Variable *Y*.

be able to predict specific criterion values very efficiently from the test scores. If we could, there would be very little variation in scores within any one of the columns; or, stated differently, all scores in any column would tend to be located very close together.

Although the correlation coefficient states the extent to which values of one variable tend to change systematically with changes in value of a second variable, correlation is not evidence of causation. Two variables may be related without either one *causing* change in the other. Thus:

> Among elementary school pupils, there is a positive correlation between length of index finger and mental age. In other words, the longer the index finger, the higher the mental age. Before you start using length of index finger as a test of intelligence (or begin to stretch your child's finger), wait a minute! Do you suppose that higher intelligence causes the longer finger, or vice versa? Neither, of course. Among elementary school children, higher *chronological* ages result both in higher mental ages and in longer fingers.

As mentioned earlier, we shall consider here only the Pearson product-moment correlation coefficient (r) and the Spearman rank-difference correlation coefficient (rho, ρ). The product-moment correlation is computed when both variables are measured continuously and certain specified assumptions can be made. The rank-difference correlation may be employed when the data are expressed as ranks, rather than scores; rank coefficients (there are others beside Spearman's) are somewhat less efficient, but often are reasonably good estimates of r. The formulas for these two types of correlation are given here only for the sake of illustration:

$$r_{xy} = \frac{\Sigma(X - \overline{X})(Y - \overline{Y})}{Ns_x s_y}$$

where r_{xy} = product-moment correlation coefficient
Σ = "add the values of"
X = raw score on Variable X
$\overline{X}$ = mean of Variable X
Y = raw score on Variable Y
$\overline{Y}$ = mean of Variable Y
N = number of pairs of scores
s_x = standard deviation of Variable X
s_y = standard deviation of Variable Y,

and

$$\rho = 1 - \frac{6\Sigma D^2}{N(N^2 - 1)}$$

where ρ = rank-difference correlation coefficient
Σ = "add the values of"
D = difference between a person's rank on Variable X and Variable Y
N = number of cases

Correlation methods demand that we have a pair of scores for each individual.

We want to find a validity coefficient of the hypothetical *Industrial Index* by correlating its scores with criterion values (number of units produced during a four-hour period of work). We have test scores for seventy-nine people and criterion information on seventy-four people. The greatest number on whom we could possibly compute our correlation coefficient would be seventy-four; however, if some of the seventy-four people did not take the test we will have an even smaller number with which to work.

Correlation coefficients are widely used in testing to express validity (where test scores are correlated with criterion values) and reliability (where two sets of scores for the same test are correlated).

THE NORMAL PROBABILITY CURVE

So far we have been discussing obtained distributions of test scores. Now it is time to consider a theoretical distribution: the normal probability distribution, the graphic representation of which is known to us as the *normal curve* (see Figure 4.8). We will never obtain a distribution exactly like it, for it is based on an infinite number of observations which vary by pure mathematical assumptions than the mean. Although less widely used than the mean, it is easily understood and easily computed.

The mode is less widely used than either the mean or the median. It provides a quick and easy estimate of central tendency, but it is not especially useful in connection with test scores.

There are still other measures of central tendency, but none is commonly used in testing. Any measure of central tendency can be located as a *point* along the abscissa of a graph.

Measures of Variability

It is possible for two distributions of scores to have a similar (even identical) central tendency value and yet be very different. The scores in one distribution, for example, may be spread over a far greater range of values than those in the other distribution. These statistics tell us how much variability (or dispersion) there is in a distribution; that is, they tell us how scattered the scores are. In graphic work, each variability measure is shown as a *distance* along the baseline.

1. Range

The *range* is familiar to all of us, representing the difference between the highest and lowest scores. The range is easily found and easily understood, but is valuable only as a rough indication of variability. It is the least stable measure of variability, depending entirely on the two most extreme (and, therefore, least typical) scores. It is less useful in connection with other statistics than other measures of variability.

2. Semi-interquartile range

This statistic defines itself: *semi* (half) *inter* (between) *quartile* (one of three points dividing the distribution into four groups of equal size) *range* (difference or distance). The statistic equals one-half the distance between the extreme quartiles, Q_3 (seventy-fifth percentile) and Q_1 (twenty-fifth percentile).

We use the semi-interquartile range (or quartile deviation) as a measure of dispersion whenever we use the median as the measure of central tendency. It is preferred to other measures when a distribution of scores is truncated or badly skewed. The formula for the semi-interquartile range is:

$$Q = \frac{Q_3 - Q_1}{2}$$

where Q = semi-interquartile range
Q_3 = third quartile, the seventy-fifth percentile (P_{75})
Q_1 = first quartile, the twenty-fifth percentile (P_{25})

3.   *Average deviation (mean deviation)*

Another statistic which has been used to express variability is the average deviation or mean deviation. Its chief advantage is the simplicity of its rationale, for it is simply the mean *absolute* amount by which scores differ from the mean score; however, it is seldom used today. It is mentioned *only* because there are occasional references to it in testing literature.

4.   *The standard deviation*

Although its rationale is less obvious than in other measures of variability, the *standard deviation* is the best such measure. It is the most dependable measure of variability, for it varies less than other measures from one sample to the next. It fits mathematically with other statistics. It is widely accepted as the best measure of variability and is of special value to test users because it is the basis for (1) standard scores; (2) a way of expressing the reliability of a test score; (3) a way of indicating the accuracy of values predicted from a correlation coefficient; and (4) a common statistical test of significance. This statistic, in short, is one which *every test user should know thoroughly.*

The standard deviation is equal to the square root of the mean of the squared deviations from the distribution's mean. Although more efficient computational formulas exist for the standard deviation, the following formula is descriptive:

$$s_x = \sqrt{\frac{\Sigma (X - \overline{X})^2}{N}}$$

where s_x = standard deviation of Test X
$\sqrt{}$ = "take the square root of"
Σ = "add the values of"
X = raw score on Test X
$\overline{X}$ = mean of Test X
N = number of persons whose scores are involved

What does the standard deviation mean? As a measure of variability it can be expressed as a distance along the baseline of a graph. The standard deviation is often used as a unit in expressing the difference between two specified score values; differences expressed in this fashion are more comparable from one distribution to another than they would be if expressed as raw scores.

The standard deviation is also frequently used in making interpretations from the normal curve (described later in this chapter). In a normal distribution, 34.13 percent of the area under the curve lies between the mean and a point that is one standard deviation away from it; 68.26 percent of the area lies between a point that is one standard deviation below the mean and a point one standard deviation above the mean. In nonnormal distributions (and perfect normality is never achieved in practice), the figure will not be exactly 68.26 percent but it will be approximately that percentage. In other words, approximately two-thirds of the area (and two-thirds of the cases, for area represents number of persons) will fall within one standard deviation of the mean in most distributions; approximately one-third of the cases will be more than one standard deviation away from the mean.

5. Probable error (PE)

The probable error is rarely used today, but it is mentioned frequently in older testing literature. It is found by multiplying the standard deviation by the constant value, 0.6745; that is, $PE_x = 0.6745 \ s_x$. Back when few people understood even basic statistics, writers used the *PE* to determine the points ($\pm$ 1 *PE* from the mean) between which fall 50 percent of the cases and beyond which fall 50 percent of the cases *in a normal distribution*.

The probable error has only this explanatory use. The *PE* does not combine with other measures—as does the standard deviation—and the standard deviation must be computed before the *PE* can be found.

Measures of Covariability

Measures of *covariability* tell us the extent of the relationship between two tests (or other variables). There is a wide variety of correlation methods, but we shall consider only two of them here: the Pearson product-moment correlation coefficient and the Spearman rank-difference correlation coefficient.

Correlation is the degree of relationship between two (or, in specialized techniques, even more) variables. A correlation coefficient is an index number expressing the degree of relationship; it may take any value from 0.00 (no relationship) to + 1.00 (perfect positive correlation) or − 1.00 (perfect negative correlation). Let us take three extreme (and impractical) examples to illustrate correlation.

In Figure 4.6(a) we see a perfect positive correlation. Ten students have taken a math test. Their scores are shown as Number Right across the abscissa and as Percent Right along the ordinate. Each dot in this scatter diagram represents one student's score according to both Number Right and Percent Right. Since there is a perfect correlation, the dots fall along a straight line. Since the correlation is positive, the dots proceed from lower left to upper right.

In Figure 4.6(b) we see a perfect negative correlation. Here we have the same ten students with their test scores as Number Right (across the abscissa) and Number Wrong (along the ordinate). The dots fall along a straight line, but proceed from upper left to lower right as is characteristic of negative correlations.

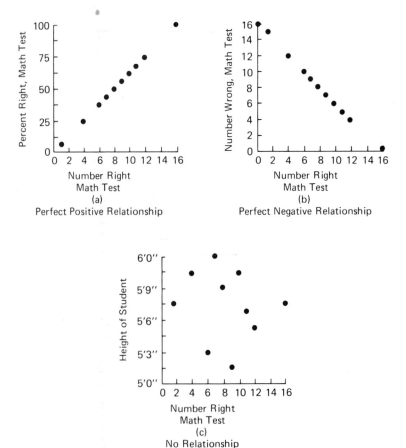

FIGURE 4.6.   Scatter Diagrams Showing Different Relationships Between Two Variables.

There is no regular order to the dots in Figure 4.6(c), for this is a correlation coefficient of 0.00—no correlation at all, neither positive nor negative. Once again, the Number Right is shown along the abscissa, but this time we have shown Height of Student along the ordinate. Apparently, there is no tendency for math scores and heights to be related.

We never encounter a perfect correlation in actual practice. Only rarely are we likely to encounter any correlation coefficients above 0.90 except as reliability coefficients (see "Reliability" in Chapter 3). Validity coefficients (see "Validity" in Chapter 3) are much more likely to run between about 0.20 and 0.60 depending upon the test, the criterion, and the variability in scores within the group tested.

Figure 4.7 shows a correlation coefficient of approximately 0.50. This is the sort of scatter diagram we might reasonably expect to find for the correlation between a test and its criterion; in fact, such a correlation may be a reasonably good validity coefficient. Note, however, that we would not

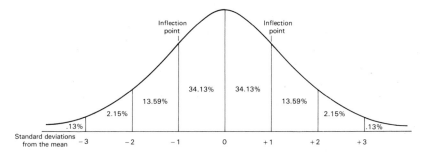

FIGURE 4.8. The Normal Probability Curve.

chance. Nevertheless, many human characteristics do seem to be distributed in much this way, and most tests yield distributions which approximate this model when given to large numbers of people.

When our results are not grossly asymmetrical, we find it convenient to treat variables as if they were normally distributed because all the properties of this mathematical model are known. If different obtained distributions approach this same model, we have a better basis for comparisons than we otherwise would have.

The normal curve is important, then, because (1) it is a mathematical model whose properties are known completely; (2) it is a model that is approached by the distributions of many human characteristics and most test scores; (3) it is relevant to an understanding of certain inferential statistics; and (4) it gives a basis for understanding the relationship between different types of test scores.

Points to Know

Chart 4.1 and Figure 4.8 constitute a summary of information about the normal probability curve that every test user should know. These points are worth remembering—even if we have to memorize them!

INFERENTIAL STATISTICS

Inferential statistics (sometimes called *sampling* statistics or *probability* statistics) tell us how much confidence may be placed in our descriptive statistics. Whereas descriptive statistics are values used to summarize a set of values, inferential statistics are used to answer the question "So what?" about descriptive statistics. They can be used to tell whether a descriptive statistic based on only a *sample* of cases is likely to be a close estimate of the value we would find for the entire *population*, or whether the observed difference between means for two groups is probably due to something other than mere chance, and so on.

CHART 4.1

In the normal probability curve:

1. The curve is bilaterally symmetrical; that is, the left and right halves are mirror images of each other. (Therefore the mean and median have the same value.)

2. The curve is highest in the middle of the distribution. (Therefore the mode is equal to the mean and the median.)

3. The limits of the curve are plus and minus infinity. (Therefore the tails of the curve will never quite touch the baseline.)

4. The shape of the curve changes from convex to concave at points one standard deviation above and one below the mean.

5. About 34% (34.13%) of the total area under the curve lies between the mean and a point one standard deviation away. (Since area represents number of cases, about 34% of the examinees have scores which fall between the mean and a point one standard deviation away.)

6. Nearly 48% (47.72%) of the area (nearly 48% of the cases) lies between the mean and a point two standard deviations away.

7. Nearly 49.9% (49.87%) of the area (and the cases) lies between the mean and a point three standard deviations away.

8. About 68% (68.26%) of the area (and the cases) lies within one standard deviation (plus and minus) of the mean. (This was found by doubling the 34% in item 5, above. In the same way, the percentages in items 6 and 7 may be doubled to find the percentage of area or cases lying within two and three standard deviations of the mean, respectively.)

9. A known mathematical formula describes the curve exactly.

10. Tables exist giving all sorts of information: height of the ordinate at any distance (in standard-deviation units) from the mean, percentage of total area between any two points, etc.

Standard Errors

Although we won't give here a detailed treatment of inferential statistics, we must develop one concept: the *standard error* (especially, the standard error of measurement).

Every descriptive statistic has its standard error. *A standard error is an estimate of the standard deviation of a distribution of like statistics*; it expresses how much variation we might expect if we were to compute the same statistic on other groups similar to the one with which we are working.

Although the formulas for standard error vary according to the statistic, most standard errors become smaller (which is what we want) when the number of cases is large and when there is little variability in a set of scores (or a high correlation between sets of scores).

1. Standard error of measurement

The standard error of measurement (SE_{meas}) indicates how much we would expect a person's score to vary if examined repeatedly with the same test (assuming that no learning occurs). The standard error of measurement is one way of expressing a test's reliability. As test users, we do not have to compute this statistic ourselves—unless, perhaps, we want to verify that the SE_{meas} for our group is comparable to that reported by the test publisher.

According to measurement theory, when one person takes the same test an infinite (or very large) number of times, the result will be a distribution of obtained scores that (1) is normal in shape; (2) has a mean equal to the person's *true* score; and (3) has a standard deviation that is estimated by the standard error of measurement.

But in any practical situation, we have only one obtained score for a person. We may think of that score as being an estimate of the true score (even though the *true* score is never determinable). We can now answer such a question as *How much is this person's score likely to differ from the true score?*

We answer the question by using our knowledge of the normal curve, the person's obtained score, and the size of the standard error of measurement—found from this formula:

$$SE_{meas} = s_x \sqrt{1 - r_{xx}}$$

where SE_{meas} = standard error of measurement
s_x = standard deviation of Test X
$\sqrt{}$ = "take the square root of"
r_{xx} = a reliability coefficient for Test X

We know that 68 percent of all cases lie between points 1 standard deviation above and 1 standard deviation below the mean. It follows that the probability is 0.68 and that our one obtained score is no more than ± 1 SE_{meas} away from the true score (that is, the mean of the theoretical distribution of scores). Similarly, the probability is 0.95 that the obtained score is no further than ± 1.96 SE_{meas} from that mean.

When we focus our interest on a range of score values within which the true score is most likely to be, we are creating a *confidence interval*; the score values at the two extremes are *confidence limits*. Thus, the 95 percent confidence interval extends from 1.96 SE_{meas} above to 1.96 SE_{meas} below the obtained score; the score values at $+1.96$ SE_{meas} and at -1.96 SE_{meas} are the 95 percent confidence limits.

Following this line of reasoning, we can set up whatever confidence limits seem reasonable. If we want to be extremely certain of the value of any score that we attribute to a counselee, we may use the 99 percent confidence limits; however, very often we are more interested in suggestions that may be gained from the various tests we've had the counselee take. In such instances, I have found it helpful to use something like a 90 percent confidence interval. This, it seems to me, is a good compromise between being too rigid and too lax. Actually, I use $\pm 1.6\ SE_{\text{meas}}$ instead of $\pm 1.65\ SE_{\text{meas}}$ because of easier multiplication.

Let's take an example:

> Margot makes a score of 73 on an aptitude test. *How close is this to her true score?* We can't tell exactly, but we can gain some information. First, Margot's obtained score (the only one we have) of 73 is the best estimate of her true score. Second, through the use of confidence limits we can state the probability of the true score being within any given distance from that obtained score.
>
> Thus, if we use the 90 percent confidence interval with Margot's score of 73, we can say that we are about 90 percent certain that her true score falls within the interval: $73 \pm 1.6\ SE_{\text{meas}}$. Assume that the test has a standard error of measurement of 2.5. We multiply: $1.6 \times 2.5 = 4.0$. Thus, the confidence interval would be 73 ± 4, or 69 to 77. We can have reasonable confidence that Margot's true score falls within that interval.

The standard error of measurement is extremely important for test users. If we assume that a person's obtained score is necessarily the true score, we will make all kinds of misinterpretations.

> Willie and Wallie White are brothers. Willie's IQ, found on a group test taken in the second grade, was 108. Wallie's IQ, found on the same test when he was in the second grade, was 111. Willie's score was interpreted as *average*, but Wallie's score was described as *above average*. According to many IQ classifications, we might very well describe these two IQs in this fashion. We should note, however, that no test scores are perfect, and that it is entirely possible that the theoretical true scores of Willie and Wallie on this test would place them in the reverse order.

Those of us who teach know the difficulty we often have in deciding exactly where to draw the line between A and B grades, B and C grades, and so on. It is probable that *true* appraisals (if available) would reverse the grades of many borderline students. This same situation exists with every type of score.

1. *Errors, not necessarily mistakes*

When we speak of error here, we are speaking of the error that is inherent in any measurement. It is something with which we must cope whenever we have a continuous variable.

Mistakes can be guarded against. But the error of measurement we are considering here is always with us. We cannot eliminate measurement error, but we can estimate how much error is present. We can eliminate mistakes, but we cannot estimate their extent when they are present.

Because of certain similarities, the standard error of measurement is often confused with the standard error of estimate, the only other standard error that we'll mention.

2. *Standard error of estimate (SE_{yx})*

The purpose of the standard error of estimate is to indicate how well test scores predict criterion values. Correlation coefficients give us the basis for predicting values of a criterion from our knowledge of obtained test scores. The SE_{yx} shows how much our obtained criterion values are likely to differ from those predicted. With a perfect correlation (± 1.00), we can predict perfectly; the SE_{yx} will equal 0.00, for there will be no difference between predicted and obtained criterion values. With no correlation between the test and the criterion, we can assume that everyone will fall at the mean on the criterion, and we will be less wrong in doing this than we would be in making any other sort of prediction. But the SE_{yx} now will be as large as the standard deviation.

Most SE_{yx}, of course, fall between these two extremes. (This concept is developed thoroughly in statistics texts, and I'll make no effort to do so here.)

We find that we need very high correlations for predicting specific values with much accuracy; however, we can make general predictions very effectively with the modest-sized validities which we typically find. Consider the following example adapted from The Psychological Corporation's *Test Service Bulletin No. 45*:

> In a given company, seventy-four stenographers were given The Psychological Corporation's *Short Employment Tests (SET)*. Each stenographer was rated by a supervisor as low, average, or high in ability. The valid coefficient (based on these ratings) was just 0.38, so there would be little predictive efficiency, according to the standard error of estimate.

TABLE 4.3* Percentage Of Stenographers In Each Third On SET-Clerical Who Earned Various Proficiency Ratings

SET-CLERICAL TEST SCORE	PROFICIENCY RATING		
	LOW	AVERAGE	HIGH
Upper Third	18	33	50
Middle Third	29	36	28
Lower Third	53	31	22
Total Percentage	100	100	100
Number of Stenographers	17	39	18

*Adapted from The Psychological Corporation's *Test Service Bulletin No. 45, "Better than Chance"* (1953). (Used with permission.)

Let us see what happens if we try to predict which employees will fall into which criterion categories instead of the specific criterion values we were concerned with in earlier examples. Table 4.3 shows for each criterion category the percentage of stenographers in each third on the Clerical part of the *SET*. The late Alexander Wesman, author of the *Bulletin*, states:

> By chance alone, the percent of upper, middle, and low scorers in each of the rated groups would be the same—in this case, 33-1/3%. The boldface numbers in the table would consist of nine 33s. Note how closely this expected percent is approximated for those ranked average in proficiency, and for those in the middle third on test score; the percentages in the middle row and those in the middle column run between 28 and 36. Note also that at the extremes—the four corner numbers—the prediction picture is more promising. Among those rated low, there are almost three times as many people from the lowest third on the test as there are from the top third. Among those rated high, the percent from the top third on the test is almost two and one-half times as great as the percent from the bottom third. The personnel man would do well to be guided by these data in selecting future stenographers, even though the validity coefficient is just 0.38.
>
> The data in the above example are based on relatively small numbers of cases (which is typically true of practical test situations) and the percents found in each category are consequently somewhat unstable. The validity coefficients based on groups of such sizes are, of course, also less stable than coefficients based on large numbers of cases. The wise test user will make several validity studies using successive groups. Having done so, he may take an average of the validity coefficients from these studies as being a more dependable estimate of the validity of the test in his situation.[1]

EXPECTANCY TABLES

Table 4.3 is an expectancy table—that is, a table showing the relationship between test-score intervals and criterion categories. Typically, intervals of test scores are shown at the left of the table, the number of intervals depending partly on the number of cases involved and partly on the degree of differentiation desired for the situation. Criterion categories are usually shown across the top of the table, the number of categories here also depending on the number of cases and on the degree of differentiation desired.

Into the individual cells of the table are placed either the number of cases or the percentage of cases which fall into that score interval and criterion category; most people prefer to use percentages, feeling that this practice is easier to interpret.

Although still not too widely used in test interpretation, the expectancy table is an excellent device to use when communicating test results to laymen. It is easy to understand and to explain to others. It

[1]The Psychological Corporation, *Test Service Bulletin No. 45* (1953).

directs attention to the purpose of testing by comparing test scores with criterion performance. (Note also the similarity to "Norms" in Chapter 5.)

Furthermore, the expectancy table is an aid in test interpretation that shows a realistic outlook so far as criterion results are concerned. A common *misinterpretation* of test scores goes something like this: "This score means that you will fail in college." No test score (except, perhaps, a final examination in some course) means any such thing. The expectancy table encourages different kinds of interpretation: "In the past, students with scores like yours have seldom succeeded at our college; in fact, only two students in ten have had satisfactory averages at the end of their first year." The latter type of interpretation can be supported; the former cannot.

Wesman has pointed out that the same general principle can be extended to two (or even more) predictor variables. (See The Psychological Corporation's *Test Service Bulletin No. 56*, 1966.)

When interpreting the results of an expectancy table, we should keep these points in mind:

1. We need to be certain that we are using the same test (including same form, level, edition, etc.).
2. The table is based on results that have been found in the past; it may or may not be relevant to the present group (or individual).
3. If the table is based on the performance of people from another office (company, school, or college), it may (or may not) apply to ours.
4. We can have more confidence in expectancy tables which are based on large numbers of scores. (Percentages sometimes disguise small numbers.)
5. Even with no special training in testing or statistics, we can make expectancy tables of our own very easily. (Several issues of The Psychological Corporation's *Test Service Bulletin** contain excellent suggestions written by the late Alexander G. Wesman; see especially *Bulletins Nos. 38 and 56*.)
6. An expectancy table may be used to spot individuals (or subgroups) that do not perform as we would expect; by noting instances in which predictions miss, we may check back to discover possible reasons for the failure.
7. In a sense we may think of an expectancy table as a set of norms in which one's test score is compared with the performance of others who have made that same score.
8. The use of double-entry expectancy table permits the simultaneous display of relationships among two predictor variables and a criterion.

**Test Service Bulletins* may be obtained for $2.00 each from The Psychological Corporation, 7500 Old Oak Boulevard, Cleveland, Ohio 44130.

AN OMISSION AND AN EXPLANATION

There are many more inferential statistics that well-trained test users should know if they are to read the testing literature or conduct research with tests. They should know that there are standard errors of differences, statistical tests of significance, and the like. But such topics are not essential to an understanding of psychological and educational test scores, and I have chosen to omit them for that reason.

Some readers may be surprised that I included expectancy tables in this chapter on statistics. I placed the topic in this chapter because I felt that a logical basis for expectancy tables had been developed in the brief discussion of the standard error of estimate.

5 ‖ THE TEST MANUAL

Where does one look for information about a specific test? The test manual is the best single source.

THE TEST CATALOG

Some people confuse the test catalog and the test manual. The catalog is a listing of the tests and test-related items which are sold by a company. The amount of detail varies considerably with the publisher. Several companies issue fancy, large-page catalogs. Others publish modest little leaflets. Whatever its appearance, the catalog should contain the following information for each test listed:

1. Title of test, including form designation.
2. Name(s) of author(s).
3. Level of persons for whom the test is appropriate.
4. Different scores available from the test (at least the titles of the subtests or subareas for which different scores are obtained—as, for example, on the *Wechsler Adult Intelligence Scale-Revised:* Verbal IQ, Performance IQ, and Full-Scale IQ).

5. Eligibility for purchase and use. [The American Psychological Association suggests a classification of A, B, or C. Level A tests are those having no specific requirements beyond an ability to read and follow directions (for example, simple paper-and-pencil tests of proficiency and achievement); Level B tests require some training in testing (such as simple adjustment or interest inventories, paper-and-pencil intelligence and aptitude tests, etc.); and Level C tests require extensive relevant training (such as individual tests of intelligence or personality).]

6. Length of time required for administration and scoring.

7. Availability of (or necessity for) using a special scoring service. Some tests can be scored only by a special service.

8. The formats in which the test, answer sheets, and other test-related materials are available. For example, the *Minnesota Multiphasic Personality Inventory* is used sometimes in a card form, but more commonly in one or another of several booklet forms; some tests may be purchased in either consumable or reusable test booklet forms and may be used with several different answer sheets that may be hand scored or machine scored.

9. Need for special equipment. Individual intelligence tests almost always require a special kit of equipment. Some instruments, such as the Rorschach inkblots, may require separate books for efficient interpretation.

10. Prices, instructions for ordering, etc.

In short, the catalog is the publication on which a publisher relies to make people aware of the products and services the company has for sale. The test publisher has an obligation to describe them briefly and accurately. The publisher has no obligation to give an extended and detailed description of the test and how it can be used, for such material belongs in the manual.

TEST PUBLISHERS

Test publishers are unique people: they must adhere to professional ethics while competing actively in the world of business. With more than one million tests being used each school day in American schools alone, testing is big business!

But, competitive as test publishing is, the publishers are expected to adhere to a code of professional ethics. And most publishers do. They are expected, for example, to accept orders only from qualified purchasers. No law prohibits—or even restricts—the sale of the *Stanford-Binet* or the *Thematic Apperception Test* or the *California Psychological Inventory* or the *Kaufman Assessment Battery for Children*, but the publishers will sell them only to qualified professionals. The integrity of all tests depends on the integrity of the people who publish and sell them. Most publishers prove worthy of the trust. In fact, reputable publishers will even recommend the products of another publisher when appropriate.

MANUALS

Once upon a time . . . there was a day when the test publisher issued a manual, and that was that! The manual was a tiny leaflet which included some directions for administering and scoring the test, together with a set of norms. And that single set of norms might be based on just one or two hundred people—with no real clue given as to whom they might be.

But those days are gone forever. Test publishers are sophisticated enough to know that a good test manual should contain a great deal more information. Further, and more important, test users realize that more information is needed.

Progress certainly has been made, but not without bringing problems of its own. There are complete manuals (or handbooks), manuals for administration and scoring, manuals for interpretation, technical manuals and supplements, and so on.

Years ago the leaflet-manual was included free of charge with each package of twenty-five test booklets. The complete manuals of today may run to more than one hundred pages—and are no longer giveaway items.

The good manual is likely to be an impressive book, full of tables, statistical formulas, and technical data. It's so imposing, in fact, that it can alarm the casual user. Thus, the paradox: the better a publisher succeeds in preparing a manual that is reasonably complete, the more overwhelming it may seem to be.

The good manual should include at least the following in addition to full identification of the test and its authors:

1. Rationale: what the test is all about.
2. Description of the test.
3. Purposes for which the test seems appropriate.
4. Development of the test, including items.
5. Directions for administration.
6. Directions for scoring.
7. Reliability data.
8. Validity data.
9. Norms tables.
10. Interpretation of the test.
11. Profiles.
12. Bibliography.

In some tests there is need for additional sorts of information. The achievement test may require an explanation of the items and perhaps item analysis data. The aptitude battery may require information about the intercorrelation of the several tests in the battery. The test that is available in alternate forms requires evidence that the forms yield similar results. *Et cetera.*

With so much information needed about any test that is published for widespread use, there are always many people involved in the development and standardization of the test, from its original planning and item writing, to the eventual establishment of norms and suggestions for interpretation; however, most tests still are identified with the individual(s) most responsible. I like to see test authors clearly identified.

Rationale

Most good test manuals contain a statement of the orientation of the test author. What is the author trying to accomplish?

Some tests have little need for any detailed statement. One sentence may be enough: "The *Wesman Personnel Classification Test (PCT)* measures the two most generally useful aspects of mental ability—verbal reasoning and numerical ability," according to The Psychological Corporation's 1965 manual for the *PCT*. On the other hand, the same publisher devotes nine pages to "The Rationale of the Children's Scale" in its manual for the *Wechsler Intelligence Scale for Children—Revised* (1974); even then, it is noted that further details on the late David Wechsler's views on the nature of intelligence are found among his other publications. If the test differs in major ways from other tests, the author and publisher need to explain what is new and different. If the test is for a familiar and common use (such as in the selection of clerical employees), there is less need for an extensive statement.

Description of Tests

Here, too, the amount of detail needed depends on a variety of factors such as familiarity or novelty of the variables, number of variables reported, and so on. On typical-performance tests, the descriptions are usually brief paragraphs explaining what each variable means.

Obviously there is less need for detailed descriptions of the test variables if there has been an extensive treatment of the rationale, or, perhaps, the interpretation of scores. In the description of an achievement battery, the test publisher should include a content analysis—a detailed statement of the number of items which are designed to measure each subtopic.

Purposes of the Test

Here again, how much needs to be said about the purposes for which the test may be used depends on the test and on how much of the information has been stated elsewhere in the manual. Regardless of how the information is labeled, the manual should contain somewhere a clear statement of the purposes the publisher believes that the test will serve.

Development of the Test

Test publishers vary widely in the attention they give to explaining the research underlying the test. Some are most admirable; some, very deficient. Most of the better-known achievement batteries have manuals containing comprehensive and detailed statements of development. Usually publishers are extremely careful to describe the research evidence that makes the current edition comparable to previous editions. Also, they give full details about the comparability of any alternate forms.

Regardless of the type of test, the user has a right to expect suitable details of the research involved in its development. This is especially true where there is little evidence of criterion-related validity.

Directions for Administration

Some publishers are careless about the directions for administration. They've been in testing for so long that they forget that there are always newcomers to testing. You and the test publisher and I may know that we need to plan ahead of time whenever we're giving a test—plan to make certain that we have all of the necessary materials, that we have reserved the right room for the right time, that all clearances have been made with school or plant officials, and that all examinees know where they are to be, and when, and for what purpose.

We may know, but there are newcomers who need to be told. The thoughtful publisher remembers them and includes a section which may be labeled "Preparing for the Test" or "General Directions."

General instructions for test administration are also needed in manuals for individual tests; but the emphasis there characteristically is on the need for establishing and maintaining rapport (a good testing relationship with the examinee), details of test administration, and the like. For example, more than twenty pages of *The Stanford-Binet Intelligence Scale*[2] (the official title of the *Stanford-Binet* manual) deal with *general* directions for administering the test; many more, of course, are needed for the *specific* directions.

There are now so many different ways of scoring tests that there may be (as we noted earlier) several different types of answer sheets on which the test may be taken. When options exist, the examiner needs to note carefully whether there are different directions to be followed for each type of answer sheet. There should be—and the differences may be more important than mere differences in how to make marks on the answer sheets.

If, for example, any parts of a test are timed, it may make a considerable difference which answer sheet is used; this is most true whenever the test is genuinely speeded (long enough so that a substantial number of the

---

[2]*The Stanford-Binet Intelligence Scale,* Boston: Houghton Mifflin Company, 1973.

examinees will not finish). If there are truly no differences in results, the manual should cite the experimental results to justify the interchangeable answer sheets.

Directions for Scoring

If there are different types of answer sheets which may be used, the manual must explain the procedure for handling each one. As noted above, it is sometimes possible to hand-score tests even when machine-scorable answer sheets have been used. The manual should explain this, too.

Because of the increasing usage of commercial scoring services, the manual should indicate the availability of such scoring services—and should indicate, whenever applicable, the procedures to follow in preparing and shipping answer sheets to such service centers.

Reliability Data

Reliability is such a complex topic that no manual can dismiss it by such a statement as: "The reliability of the test is 0.89." The good manual considers the following questions (and many others): What type of reliability? What sort of group? Why are these estimates of reliability appropriate? One manual for the *Differential Aptitude Tests* spent about ten pages on the discussion of reliability. The authors listed reliability coefficients separately by sex and by grade, for each form, and for each of the tests in the battery. There are split-half coefficients, test-retest coefficients, and alternate-form coefficients. In addition, there are standard errors of measurement for each sex and each grade for each of the tests.

Validity Data

When the test is a simple, job-oriented aptitude test, the statement of validity can be fairly straightforward. The manual can state criterion-related validity coefficients, both predictive and concurrent, for various groups. These, when well and appropriately accomplished, may be sufficient for such tests.

With other tests, there is greater need for more consideration of validity data. Let's take a look at the common achievement battery. There is no good criterion; the standardized tests should do a better job than informal, teacher-made tests, and there is little likelihood that the standardized tests were designed to parallel exactly the teacher-made tests, anyway. Part of the validity data may be correlation coefficients between the achievement tests and corresponding course achievement, but more is needed.

With achievement tests, publishers tend to lean heavily on evidence of content validity, that is, evidence of agreement between content of test items and content of courses and textbooks. For example, in the *Cooperative Primary Tests,* the Educational Testing Service includes information about the percentage of children in the norms groups selecting each alternative of each item. In this way we may study the percentage of pupils at each grade placement which answered the item correctly.

Similar evidence is sometimes cited for intelligence tests. Items for the *Stanford-Binet Scales of Intelligence* have been selected partly on the basis of their ability to discriminate among children of different ages.

Another evidence of validity that is found in many manuals takes the form of correlations with other tests. This sort of evidence, although rarely sufficient, often is valuable supplementary evidence. After all, if the only evidence of validity is that the test relates to some other test, what are we to infer? Is the other test sufficiently valid that we may accept it immediately? Then why not use that other test?

Correlations with other tests, as used with the *Differential Aptitude Tests (DAT)*, can be of great help in deciding whether another test is sufficiently different to justify our using both of them or whether it would be sufficient, perhaps, to use just one. Such correlations are also helpful in determining the exact nature of the test variable. The fifth edition of the manual for the *DAT* contains eight pages of correlations with other tests. To be maximally informative, of course, these other-test correlation coefficients must include the tests of various publishers, not just one's own.

Construct validity data may take almost any form. Inasmuch as personality and intelligence tests do not adapt well to criterion-related validity, evidence must usually be sought through construct validity. What group differences should be obtained if the test has good validity? What other variables can give evidence of the test's validity?

Differences between age groups and the like are commonly used as evidence of validity of tests for school use. Similar reasoning can be used with occupational groups, as has been done by The Psychological Corporation with the *Wesman Personnel Classification Test*. The logic is that if the test possesses high validity, there should be reasonable order to the means for the various occupations. The following data suggest that the *PCT* may have validity for use in personnel section:

TABLE 5.1*

	MEAN SCORE		
OCCUPATIONAL GROUP	VERBAL	NUMERICAL	TOTAL
Chain-store clerks	12.0	6.4	18.4
Production workers	17.1	8.2	25.3
Female clerical employees	23.0	8.9	31.9
U.S. Air Force captains	23.9	11.2	35.2
Executive trainee applicants	27.1	14.5	41.6
Technical sales applicants	29.4	14.7	44.1

*Data extracted from Table 3, *Wesman Personnel Classification Test Manual*. The Psychological Corporation (1965). The original table lists 24 different occupational groups, together with the number of cases involved in each and the standard deviation for each.

Validity is the most important attribute of a test. The manual must cite appropriate evidence that the test possesses some sort of validity. It is the test user's responsibility to evaluate the evidence that is presented—and to evaluate it in view of the use that is to be made of the test. Remember: *a test may have high validity for one purpose but have little or no validity for some other purpose.*

Norms and Norms Tables

Norms are vital to an understanding of test results, for they provide us with the standards against which to compare test performance. Most test manuals contain several sets of norms, and it is important for the reader to select the set that is most appropriate to use. As we shall see, an individual's score may show one as either doing well or doing poorly, depending on the group with which one is compared. Mitzi may have made the lowest score of all the fifth graders in her Executive Heights School, but the same score might have placed her in the highest quarter of her class if she had been attending the Bottoms District School or the Jelly Junction School.

The norm

The simplest statement of norms is given by the *norm*. This is nothing more than the average (either mean or median) score for some specified group. Norm, in fact, is used occasionally as a synonym for average. A norm is also used sometimes in place of more complete norms if the available scores are inadequate, inappropriate, or suspect for some reason. On a new test, for example, scores may be available on very few people.

A set of norms for a test consists of a table giving corresponding values of raw scores and derived scores. Derived scores are intended to make test interpretation easier and more meaningful than is possible with raw scores alone.

Norms are frequently designated according to the type of score involved; we may, for example, read of percentile norms, grade-equivalent norms, and so on. Because of the large number of different types of derived score in common use, we are devoting one entire chapter (Chapter 6) to discussing them.

Norms tables

A good *norms table* should include a derived-score equivalent for each raw score that can be made. It should include a full description of the group on which it is based. It may present one or several types of derived score, for one or several groups, for one or more tests. An incomplete norms table may be confusing to the test user.

Simple norms tables. The simplest norms tables consist of two columns, one containing raw-score values and the other containing corresponding derived-score values. Table 5.2 illustrates such a table with hypothetical results presumed to be based on a national sample of laboratory technicians. Note that the group is described in some detail. The test manual should list the laboratories which contributed data (or should note that the list is available on request). In this example, we might still ask questions about the educational background and work experience of the examinees, for these factors could influence our interpretation. Of course, if we want to use the *TAPT* for any individual decisions, we need to have a much longer test.

TABLE 5.2   Example Of Simple Norms Table (Percentile Norms For The Hypothetical Technician's Aptitude And Proficiency Test)*

RAW SCORE	PERCENTILE	RAW SCORE	PERCENTILE	RAW SCORE	PERCENTILE	RAW SCORE	PERCENTILE
11	98	8	75	5	34	2	10
10	96	7	62	4	23	1	4
9	85	6	48	3	18	0	1

*Hypothetical data. Presumably based on 6,245 laboratory technicians tested last year at 450 hospital laboratories and 785 industrial and commercial laboratories in 39 states. (The complete list of participating laboratories should be included in the manual or made available upon request.)

Multiple-group norms tables. Very often a single norms table is constructed to show results from several different groups. Besides the obvious economy in printing, this practice permits the comparison of a person's raw score with as many of these groups as we wish. Table 5.3 illustrates such a table with data drawn from Project TALENT; it is based on a 4 percent random sample of approximately 440,000 high school students tested in 1960 as part of that research study. The test we are concerned with is the *Information Test—Aeronautics and Space.* Here again there are so few items that we must be cautious in interpreting individual scores. The chance passing of one more item or chance failing of one more item makes a great apparent difference in performance.

Pauline, a ninth-grade girl, had a score of 3; this gives her a percentile rank of 65 when compared with other ninth-grade girls. Pauline knows very little about aeronautics and space, and she might easily have missed one more item; that would have placed her at the fortieth percentile. On the other hand, if she had happened to guess correctly on one or two more items than she did, she would have had a percentile rank of 83 or 93.

With very short tests such as these last two, reliability is likely to be extremely low, especially when the items are so difficult that lucky guesses become important in determining one's score. We should be very careful in making any interpretations of individual test scores here except for students clearly at one extreme or the other.

We can rely on group differences to a far greater extent. We often can have confidence in group differences in test performance even when test reliability is too low to permit much confidence in individual scores. Note that here there is no level at which youngsters in one grade have done better than those in any higher grade. Nor is there any level at which girls have done better than boys. The gender differences will be reduced as girls are given greater encouragement (and reward) in school for an interest in science.

Multiple-score norms tables. Sometimes a norms table includes derived scores for each of several tests (or subtests). For obvious reasons this should never be done unless the same *norms group* is used for each test. Sometimes scaled scores (see Chapter 6) are used instead of raw scores, especially when some of the subtests have many more items than do others.

Abbreviated norms tables. An occasional norms table includes only alternate raw-score values (or, perhaps, every fifth raw-score value), thereby forcing the test user to interpolate whenever he has a nontabled raw score. Such a table saves money in printing, but it encourages mistakes and costs the test user additional time and trouble.

Condensed norms tables. Very similar to the abbreviated table is the condensed table, where selected percentile (or other) values are given, and the corresponding raw scores shown. This style of table is still used, especially when the publisher wishes to present a large amount of data in a single table for comparison purposes.

Expectancy tables and charts

At this point we need to mention expectancy tables and charts once again (see pages 57-59 for a more complete discussion). They differ from norms tables in one important characteristic: whereas norms tables state derived-score values corresponding to each raw score, expectancy tables show criterion performance for each interval of raw scores. In all other respects, expectancy tables are the same as norms tables. We reemphasize here that expectancy tables, like norms tables, state the results found for some specified group. When interpreting anyone's score through the use of either an expectancy table or a norms table, we must consider whether the group and the situation are comparable.

TABLE 5.3 Example Of Multiple-Group Norms Table (Percentile Norms For The Information Test—Aeronautics And Space, Of The Project TALENT Test Battery)*

PERCENTILE SCORE

RAW SCORE	GRADE 9 BOY	GRADE 9 GIRL	GRADE 10 BOY	GRADE 10 GIRL	GRADE 11 BOY	GRADE 11 GIRL	GRADE 12 BOY	GRADE 12 GIRL
10	99+	99+	99	99+	99	99+	98	99+
9	97	99+	96	99+	96	99+	92	99
8	92	99+	91	99+	89	99+	84	99
7	86	99	83	99	80	99	75	98
6	78	97	73	96	69	96	63	95
5	66	93	62	92	55	91	51	89
4	52	83	47	81	41	79	36	77
3	36	65	31	62	26	61	22	59
2	20	40	16	40	14	38	11	38
1	8	18	6	18	5	16	4	16
0	2	4	1	4	1	4	1	3

*Based on a 4 percent random sample of the approximately 440,000 high school students in 50 states tested in 1960 as part of the Project TALENT study directed by John C. Flanagan. Reprinted from PROJECT TALENT COUNSELORS' TECHNICAL MANUAL FOR INTERPRETING TEST SCORES, University of Pittsburgh (1961). (Used with permission.)

Articulation of norms

A specified test may vary in edition, form, level, or any combination of these. Edition refers usually either to the *date* of publication (1986 edition) or to the *number* of editions (for example, the fifth edition). Different editions may be needed to keep test content up to date. Form refers usually to an equivalent version; that is, different forms will contain different items, but will be similar in content and difficulty. Different forms may be needed to insure test security; that is, to minimize the likelihood of test items leaking out to examinees. Different form designations may also be given when item content is identical, but scoring method is different.

Level refers usually to the age or grade placement of those for whom a specified version of the test is intended. Different levels may be needed to make subject content and item difficulty appropriate for the examinees; from three to eight levels sometimes are used to cover the range of school grades. Some tests have overlapping items for adjacent levels.

Some excellent tests exist in only a single edition, form, and level. The need for multiple versions of a test becomes greater as the test is used more widely. Thus, the need is greatest, especially for different levels, with tests designed for wide-scale administration throughout whole school systems.

With few exceptions, new editions are intended to replace and to improve upon earlier editions. There may or may not be a desire to make results from two editions directly comparable. Nearly always, however, it is important to make different forms and levels yield somewhat comparable results; the aim is to achieve articulated (neatly jointed) norms. All major publishers of tests for schools are aware of this need for articulation and all take steps toward insuring comparability. The exact procedures followed differ, and some publishers are more successful than others.

Those who use tests should check the manual carefully for evidence of articulation studies to see how comparable are the test scores from different forms and levels. This information may be found under such headings as *Articulation, Interlocking Studies,* and *Overlapping Norms.* It is more difficult to obtain reliable information about the comparability of scores from the tests of different publishers, but data from Project TALENT directed by John C. Flanagan, of the American Institutes for Research, can help to fulfill this need for anchoring norms.

Norms groups

I cannot emphasize too strongly the tremendous importance of the norms *group.* Regardless of the type of norms, we are dealing with results that are based on some group of people. But it makes a great deal of difference which group of people. Consider the hypothetical example of Alan Alexakis.

Alan Alexakis, a graduate assistant in philosophy at Athol University, answered 210 words correctly on the hypothetical *Kalimera Kulture Test* of 300 items. His raw score of 210 on the *KKT* means that he did as well as or better than:

> 99 percent of the seventh-grade pupils in the Malone Public Schools
> 92 percent of the Athol High School seniors
> 91 percent of the high school graduates in Dallas, Texas
> 85 percent of the entering freshmen at Patricia Junior College
> 70 percent of the philosophy majors at Lamia College
> 55 percent of the graduating seniors at University of Thessaloniki
> 40 percent of the graduate assistants at American College of Athens
> 15 percent of the English professors at Athol University

Although Alan's absolute performance (210 words defined correctly) remains unchanged, our impression of how well he has done will differ markedly as we change norms groups.

This illustration is extreme. Under no normal circumstances would we compare a graduate assistant's score with those of seventh-grade pupils; however, results every bit as far-fetched as these *can* be obtained in real-life situations—and results nearly as farfetched often *do* occur.

Even professional measurements people occasionally are fooled by differences in norms groups, as in the following situation:

> Two tests (scholastic aptitude and reading comprehension) put out by the same highly reputable publisher were once commonly used together in college admissions batteries. At most colleges, students tended to stand relatively higher on the scholastic aptitude test than on the reading comprehension test. The norms most commonly used were national norms prepared by the publisher and based on thousands of cases from colleges in all sections of the country. The norms could be trusted. Or could they?

The norms should not have been accepted so readily, for more select colleges (with higher admissions standards) unintentionally had been used in establishing the reading test norms. The net result was that most students who took both tests seemed to do more poorly in reading comprehension than in scholastic aptitude.

Before this difference in norms groups was generally recognized, interoffice memoranda had been exchanged at many colleges—asking why their students were so deficient in reading ability! The same sort of difficulty is encountered frequently in school testing, especially when we use tests from different publishers. The following situation shows what may happen in real-life school settings where different achievement batteries are used in different grade levels.

> Wallie Winchester's pupils are tested on the *AAB* at the end of the fifth grade; their mean grade-placement score is 5.4 (which is about one-half grade below the expected norm for her class). The same pupils took the *BAB* at the end of the fourth grade and earned a mean grade-placement score of 5.1 (very

slightly *above* the norm at that time). It looks as if Ms. Winchester has not taught much to her class, especially when these pupils take the *BAB* again at the end of their sixth grade and obtain a mean grade-placement score of 7.1 (once again slightly above the norm for their actual grade placement).

Ms. Winchester is a victim of circumstances. If pupils had taken the *AAB* at the end of the fourth grade and the *BAB* at the end of the fifth grade, they would have shown great apparent improvement during their year with her.

This same sort of situation occurs in industrial settings where test-naïve personnel workers fail to consider the differences in norms groups from test to test. "After all," they may reason, "Test Y and Test Z were both standardized on mechanical employees." And such personnel workers may ignore the fact that the "mechanical employees" used for the Test Y norms were engineering technicians, whereas those used for Test Z were machine wipers and machine-shop porters.

The list of possible mistaken inferences could be extended almost indefinitely. The point we must remember is **be sure to understand the nature of the norms groups.**

Which norms to use

Most test manuals include several norms tables. Which should we use? The obvious general answer is that we should use whichever norms are most appropriate for the individual examinee and the situation involved.

We seldom have much difficulty in selecting an appropriate set of norms to use when the test is a maximum-performance test designed for routine school use. With tests not commonly given to all pupils in a school (for example, specific aptitude tests) or tests designed primarily for out-of-school use, our selection is likely to be much more difficult. For a clerical aptitude test, we may have to decide whether John should be compared with 225 clerk-typists employed by a large insurance company, 456 applicants for clerical positions with four midwestern companies, or 839 eleventh-grade students in a secretarial sequence. The same problem exists with many tests.

In guidance situations we often decide to use several different norms groups:

Dottie Divenger has taken an art aptitude test. Her score would place her very high among non-art students and adults, high average among first-year students at an art academy, and low average among employed fashion designers. All of this information may be helpful to Dottie in deciding whether to strive for a career in art, whether to attend an art academy, or whatever.

Local norms

Local norms are sometimes better than national norms. Developing our own norms is not too difficult. We keep a careful record of the test scores made by a defined group (all applicants for some sort of position; all bookkeepers currently employed by our company; or all fourth-grade pupils in our school district) until a satisfactory number has been acquired. We arrange the scores in a frequency distribution and assign appropriate derived scores (see Chapter 6).

Circumstances help us to decide whether we should be satisfied with available national norms or whether we should develop our own. In the first place, we have no choice unless we are using the same test on a large number of people. If we use a particular test on only an occasional individual, we will have to depend on national norms because we will not have enough of our own scores to do much good.

If national norms are suitable, we have no problem. We can use them without difficulty if we want to. Yet even when the national norms are not especially appropriate, we may prefer to use them rather than to develop our own—as when it seems that nothing is to be gained by developing our own. On an interest test used for guidance purposes, for example, we may have very little to gain by comparing an individual's score with other local scores.

On the other hand, even though there are adequate national norms, there may be situations in which we would like to be able to compare individuals with other local people. We may be much more interested in knowing how well Curt compares with other local applicants than in knowing how well he has done when compared with some national normative group.

Unisex or Separate Sex?

Traditionally most tests have had separate norms for each sex. But there is increasing demand from women's groups for unisex norms. Reasons support each practice.

Where there are noticeable score differences between females and males, separate sex norms obviously are more descriptive of the test performances of the two sexes. On the other hand, it can be argued that separate-sex norms reinforce differences and tend to perpetuate any biases that may exist.

Which is better? Each test user must make an individual decision.

Assorted tests and integrated batteries

Tremendous strides have been made in psychological and educational testing during recent years. Modern-day standardized testing is not very old. Binet and Simon gave us the first acceptable intelligence test as recently as 1905. The first group intelligence test and the first personality inventory appeared during World War I. With the exception of a few standardized achievement-test batteries that emerged during the late 1920s and 1930s, almost all tests published prior to World War II were separate tests. Each new test was developed independently from every other, and very little effort was made to equate norms groups. Inevitably the test user would find results that looked like these for Meg Morner:

Percentile rank of 96 on reading speed; compared with high school students
Percentile rank of 77 on reading comprehension; compared with college freshmen
IQ of 109 on an intelligence test
IQ of 131 on another intelligence test
Standard score of 59 on clerical aptitude; compared with employed clerks
Stanine of 8 on mechanical aptitude

Under such conditions, even skilled counselors had difficulty making much sense from the results. Because each test had been developed independently by a different author, usually to meet some important need, no one could safely compare the score on one test with the score on another.

The situation has improved markedly since World War II. Several major publishers now have multiple-aptitude test batteries on which all of the tests have been standardized on the same group, with norms all based on the same group. With integrated batteries such as these, we can now make comparisons of various scores made by the same person. Has Meg done better on clerical aptitude than on reading comprehension? Better on reading speed than on mechanical aptitude? The use of tests in guidance demands answers to such questions, and with integrated test batteries we can begin to find these answers.

There are still many tests that are not part of any integrated test battery. There probably always will be. If we are concerned with selecting people (whether for employment or for training), we want to use the test (or tests) that will do the best job for us; there is no reason for us to consider whether a test is part of an integrated battery. An integrated battery of tests is most important in guidance and in differential placement, where the use of the common norms group is valuable in making comparisons of a person's relative ability within the various test areas.

It is impossible to exaggerate the value of a good norms table; the skillful test user must develop competence in studying the data in the manual.

Interpretation of the Test

Although significant technical improvements have been made in tests, I believe that the increased attention being paid to test interpretation is the biggest improvement in test manuals during the past two decades. More and more the publishers are recognizing the importance of suggesting how test users can get the most meaning out of their test results.

The Psychological Corporation has an excellent casebook for its *DAT*, *Counseling from Profiles*. Not only is the book excellent in showing how that battery may be used in counseling, it is also good in demonstrating how other information (including scores from other tests) fits in. The *DAT* interpretive folder, part of which is shown in Figures 7.1 and 7.2, is excellent.

The California Test Bureau has some excellent interpretive material, including a separate guide for its *California Test of Mental Maturity*. Science Research Associates has interpretive folders for several of its tests, most notably for the Kuder inventories. Further examples from other publishers might also be mentioned, but these are typical.

Most manuals have at least a few paragraphs illustrating how meaning can be made from the results of the test; however, it is important to remember that illustrative examples do not establish the validity of a test. Even very poor tests can be right occasionally! The proper role and function of the interpretive material is to suggest ways for using the test—not to establish the test's validity.

Profiles

The good manual contains a complete description of any profile that may be generated for a multiscore test or test battery. Chapter 7 is devoted to a more complete discussion of profiles than is possible before we have considered the various types of score (the topic of the next chapter).

Bibliography

Practices differ in the amount of bibliographic material included in the manuals. In some instances the list of references is inflated with the inclusion of statistical articles and books consulted in the preparation of validity and reliability studies. There is usually no need for any statistical or general measurements references unless new or unusual procedures have been followed.

In my opinion, there should be a list of references describing research that has been done with a test. Once again, The Psychological Corporation's *Differential Aptitude Tests* is a good example: 98 references, nearly all of them specific to research with that battery, are shown; and nearly 400 references to the *DAT* may be found in Buros' *Eighth Mental Measurement Yearbook* (Gryphon Press, 1978).

6 ‖ DERIVED SCORES

We use derived (rather than raw) scores for two reasons: (1) to make scores from different tests more comparable by expressing them in the same metric and (2) to let us make more meaningful interpretations of test results.

We need accurate raw scores in order to get accurate derived scores. No amount of statistical manipulation can make up for the use of a poor test or for mistakes in scoring. Nor does the use of derived scores reduce measurement error.

A CLASSIFICATION SCHEME

The outline shown in Chart 6.1 is an original classification showing the various sorts of score that may be used to report test results. This same information is shown in graphic form in Chart 6.2 in the belief that some testers will find it easier to appreciate the interrelationships among the score types. I hope that all readers will commit to memory the score forms represented by Type I, Type II A, B, C, D, and Type III. If we remember that much of the outline, the subtypes are much easier to understand.

CHART 6.1 *LYMAN'S CLASSIFICATION OF DIFFERENT TYPES OF TEST SCORE*

I. Comparison with "Absolute Standard"; Content Difficulty
   A. Percentage correct scores
   B. Letter grades (sometimes)

II. Inter-Individual Comparison
   A. Considering mean and standard deviation (linear standard scores)
      1. z-scores
      2. *T*-scores
      3. *AGCT*-scores
      4. *CEEB*-scores
      5. Deviation IQs (sometimes)
         (a) Wechsler IQs
         (b) Stanford-Binet IQs
   B. Considering rank within groups
      1. Ranks
      2. Percentile ranks and percentile bands
      3. Letter grades (sometimes)
      4. Decile ranks
      5. Normalized standard scores (area transformations)
         (a) *T*-scaled scores
         (b) Stanine scores
         (c) *C*-scaled scores
         (d) Sten scores
         (e) Deviation IQs (sometimes)
            (1) Wechsler subtests
         (f) *ITED*-scores
         (g) Standard age scores
         (h) Normal curve equivalents
   C. Considering range of scores in a group
      1. Percent placement
   D. Considering status of those obtaining same score
      1. Age scores
         (a) Mental ages
         (b) Educational ages, etc.
      2. Grade-placement scores

III. Intra-Individual Comparison
   A. Ratio IQs
   B. Intellectual Status Index
   C. Educational Quotients
   D. Accomplishment Quotients

IV. Assorted Arbitrary Bases
   A. Nonmeaningful scaled scores
   B. Long-range equi-unit scales
   C. Deviation IQs (Otis-style)

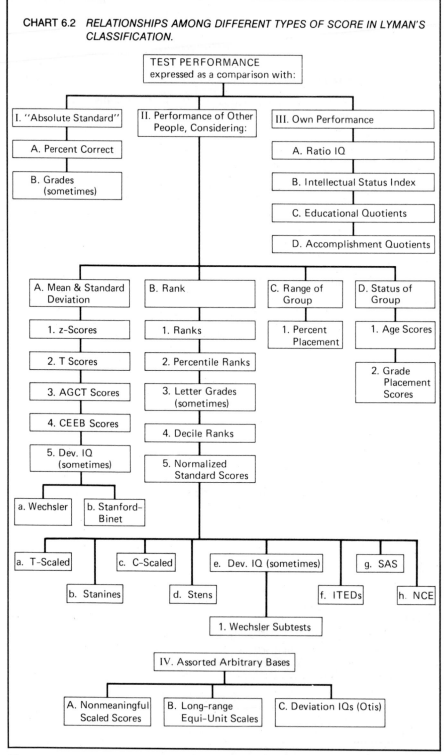

CHART 6.2 *RELATIONSHIPS AMONG DIFFERENT TYPES OF SCORE IN LYMAN'S CLASSIFICATION.*

TEST PERFORMANCE
expressed as a comparison with:

I. "Absolute Standard"

A. Percent Correct

B. Grades (sometimes)

II. Performance of Other People, Considering:

III. Own Performance

A. Ratio IQ

B. Intellectual Status Index

C. Educational Quotients

D. Accomplishment Quotients

A. Mean & Standard Deviation

1. z-Scores

2. T Scores

3. AGCT Scores

4. CEEB Scores

5. Dev. IQ (sometimes)

a. Wechsler

b. Stanford–Binet

B. Rank

1. Ranks

2. Percentile Ranks

3. Letter Grades (sometimes)

4. Decile Ranks

5. Normalized Standard Scores

C. Range of Group

1. Percent Placement

D. Status of Group

1. Age Scores

2. Grade Placement Scores

a. T-Scaled

b. Stanines

c. C-Scaled

d. Stens

e. Dev. IQ (sometimes)

1. Wechsler Subtests

f. ITEDs

g. SAS

h. NCE

IV. Assorted Arbitrary Bases

A. Nonmeaningful Scaled Scores

B. Long-range Equi-Unit Scales

C. Deviation IQs (Otis)

There are three principal bases for expressing test results: (1) comparison with an "absolute standard," or content difficulty; (2) inter-individual comparisons; and (3) intra-individual comparisons. My system centers about these three bases and a fourth (assorted) category.

In a normal distribution (see page 53), Type II A and Type II B scores are interrelated. As shown in Figure 6.1 of Chart 6.3 we can make transformations from one kind of score to another very easily if we assume a normal distribution based on the same group of individuals. Under these two assumptions, normality and same group, the relationships shown in Figure 6.1 will always exist. *When different groups are involved, we cannot make any direct comparisons; when the set of scores cannot be assumed to be distributed normally, we find that some of the relationships are changed while others still hold.*

> A certain test is given locally and is found to have a mean of 300 and a standard deviation of 40. When we notice that the distribution of scores seems to resemble closely the normal probability distribution, and we are willing to treat our set of scores as being normal, what can we say about the scores? Let us take a couple of cases and see.
>
> Bob has a raw score of 300. This would give him a z-score of 0.00, a T-score of 50, a stanine of 5, a percentile rank of 50, and so on.
>
> Patricia has a raw score of 320. This would give her a z-score of 0.5, a T-score of 55, a stanine of 6, a percentile rank of 69, and so on.

Figure 6.1 has been drawn with several baselines. Each of these can be used equally well as the graph's abscissa. To change from one type of score to another, we merely move vertically to another line.

Figure 6.2 of Chart 6.3 shows some of these same types of score in a badly skewed distribution. The sole purpose of this figure is to indicate which scores change in their relationship to others. Somewhat less detail has been shown here, for this distribution is **not** subject to generalization as is the distribution in Figure 6.1. Note that z- and *T-scores* do *not* change in their relationship to each other, nor would their relationship to raw scores change. Normalized standard scores and percentiles maintain a constant relationship to each other—but they do not relate to z- and *T-scores* (nor to raw scores) in the same manner as in the normal distribution.

Discussion of the Classification Scheme

Type I scores are the most familiar, for they are commonly used in reporting the results of classroom tests. These scores are unique in that they consider only the specified individual's performance; the performance of all other examinees is ignored in assigning the score. In a sense, Type I scores compare each examinee individually with an absolute standard of perfection (as represented by a perfect score on the test). This absolute-standard reasoning has an attractive appeal at first glance; however, thoughtful testers soon realize that the individual's score may depend more on the difficulty of the tasks presented by the test items than

CHART 6.3

Percentage of cases
under portions of
the normal curve   0.13%   2.14%   13.59%   34.13%   34.13%   13.59%   2.14%   0.13%

STANDARD
DEVIATIONS
from MEAN   −4s   −3s   −2s   −1s   0   +1s   +2s   +3s   +4s

Cumulative
Percentages   0.1%   2.3%   15.9%   50.0%   84.1%   97.7%   99.9%

Rounded   2%   16%   50%   84%   98%

PERCENTILE RANKS   1   5   10   20 30   50   70 80   90 95   99
                                   Q_1 Md Q_3

STANDARD SCORES

z − scores   −4.0   −3.0   −2.0   −1.0   0   +1.0   +2.0   +3.0   +4.0

T − scores   20   30   40   50   60   70   80

AGCT scores   40   60   80   100   120   140   160

CEEB scores   200   300   400   500   600   700   800

DEVIATION IQs
Stanford-Binet   52   68   84   100   116   132   148

Wechsler   55   70   85   100   115   130   145

CHART 6.3

ITED scores

0	5	10	15	20	25	30

STANDARD AGE SCORES						
52	68	84	100	116	132	148

STANINES

	1	2	3	4	5	6	7	8	9	
Percent in stanine	4%	7%	12%	17%	20%	17%	12%	7%	4%	

C-SCORES

0	1	2	3	4	5	6	7	8	9	10
Percent in C-score 1%	3%	7%	12%	17%	20%	17%	12%	7%	3%	1%

STENS

	1	2	3	4	5	6	7	8	9	10
Percent in sten	2%	5%	9%	15%	19%	19%	15%	9%	5%	2%

FIGURE 6.1. Relationships of selected scores in a normal distribution. Adapted from The Psychological Corporation *Test Service Bulletin No. 48* (1964). (Used with permission.)

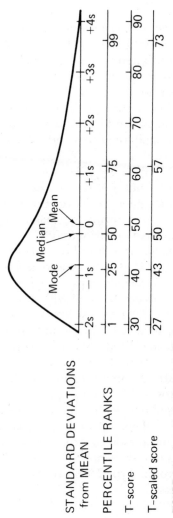

STANDARD DEVIATIONS from MEAN	−2s	−1s	0	+1s	+2s	+3s	+4s
PERCENTILE RANKS	1	25	50	75		99	
T-score	30	40	50	60	70	80	90
T-scaled score	27	43	50	57		73	

FIGURE 6.2. A positively skewed distribution.

on the individual's ability. Type I scores usually are not suited for use with standardized tests. When test scores are based on each person's own absolute level of performance, we have no way of illustrating the scores in a generalized fashion. (In other words, the mean and standard deviation are likely to differ for each test, and we have no typical distribution to illustrate.) Type I scores are *never* used with typical-performance tests; they *are* used with criterion-referenced tests.

With Type II A scores, we can show how scores are likely to be distributed for any group. Type II A scores are known as linear standard scores, and they always reflect the original distribution of raw scores; that is, if we were to draw separate graphs of the distribution of raw scores and of their standard-score equivalents, the two graphs would have identical shapes—and it would be possible to change with accuracy from raw scores to standard scores and back again. Type II A scores can be used with any sort of test.

With Type II B scores, we lose information about the shape of the distribution of raw scores unless the original distribution was normal (and of course it can never be perfectly normal). With nonnormal distributions we lose information that would be necessary to recreate the shape of the raw-score distribution; for example, when we use ranks, we lose all information as to how far apart the scores of any two examinees are. Even with Type II B scores, however, we can generalize the score systems to show what relationships always exist within a normal distribution. Type II B scores can be used with any sort of test.

Type II C scores, dependent on the two most extreme scores earned by members of a group, are more suited for use with informal than with standardized tests. The scores cannot be generalized.

With Type II D scores, the values expressed are averages of groups differing in age or in grade placement. It is impossible to generalize these scores, for they are specific to each test and group. Type II D scores can be used only with achievement or intelligence tests.

Type III scores are based on *intra*-individual comparisons, and there is no reason to expect that such scores can be generalized; therefore, we cannot show how such scores are distributed except for a specified test and group. Type III scores can be used only with achievement or intelligence tests.

Type IV scores do not fit readily into this classification scheme. They are an assortment primarily of scaled scores with more or less arbitrary values that are not intended for interpretation in themselves—that is, they are a sort of intermediate score and some other type of derived score is ordinarily provided for them.

Still another aid to understanding the similarities and differences among these scores is to be found in the Conversion Table for Derived

Scores starting on page 152. This table shows comparable values of several commonly used derived-score systems. Note carefully the explanation for using the Conversion Table (page 151).

THE SCORES

In discussing these scores, we are assuming at least a basic understanding of the mean, median, standard deviation, range, and the normal probability curve. These concepts, developed in Chapter 4, should be reviewed by the reader who feels uncertain of them.

TYPE I: COMPARISON WITH AN "ABSOLUTE STANDARD," OR CONTENT DIFFICULTY

Type I scores are suited only for maximum-performance tests and are rarely used except as scores on classroom achievement tests. One's performance on any maximum-performance test is determined in part by knowledge and skill and in part by motivation; these elements are common in determining any person's level of performance. The only other important determinants of a person's Type I score are measurement error and the difficulty of the test content, for the person's performance is being compared with perfection (that is, with the maximum-possible score on the test). The scores of other examinees play no part in determining the score of any specified examinee. Type I scores are, of course, used with criterion-referenced tests.

Type I A: Percentage Correct

The percentage-correct score often is used in reporting the results of classroom achievement tests, but is almost never used with any other type of test. It compares an examinee's score with the maximum-possible score, and it may be thought of as one's score per 100 items.

Formula:

$$X_{\%c} = 100 \ R/T$$

where $X_{\%c}$ = percentage-correct score
         R = number of right answers (items answered correctly)
         T = total number of items on test

Example: Helen Hill answers correctly 44 items on a 50-item test. Her percentage-correct score is 88. $(100 \times 44)/50 = 88$.

Percentage-correct scores are the only derived scores (except for Type I letter grades) that tell us anything about an examinee's knowledge of test content *per se*. We can understand their natural appeal to the school teacher who wants to consider what students achieve according to predetermined standards of quality. On the other hand, many teachers realize that these predetermined levels of quality are not so objective and unchanging as might be desired, for the apparent achievement level of students can be altered tremendously by writing either easier or harder test questions over the same subject-matter unit. Many experienced teachers use a *J*-factor to "jack up" scores (by adding a few points to everyone's score) when scores have been very low. Over the years many teachers have come to believe that it is more meaningful to base test scores on a system in which the performance of a student is considered in comparison with others.

Do not confuse percentage-correct scores with percentile ranks.

Type I B: Letter Grades (Sometimes)

The basis for the assignment of letter grades at most schools and colleges is stated in terms of percentage-correct scores. Thus, letter grades are one of our most common types of score. Although they may be determined on some comparative basis (Type II B 3), letter grades are commonly Type I. Often the grading system of a school or college will state something like the following: A for 90–100; B for 80–90, etc., where the numbers refer to average percentage correct on classroom tests. Some teachers have absolute faith in such a system.

The basic rationale, advantages, and limitations of letter grades are the same as for percentage-correct scores. The only important difference between these scores is that letter grades are expressed in coarser units. Because of this, letter grades cannot reflect small differences in ability; but, by the same token, they are not likely to differ greatly from hypothetical true scores. Note, however, that even a single unit of change is relatively large.

Type I letter grades are found by either of two methods: (1) direct grading according to judged quality (as is often done in grading essays) or (2) conversion from percentage-correct scores to letter grades, following a predetermined schedule, as in the school and college grading system mentioned above.

When letter grades are assigned with strict adherence to quality standards (without any consideration to relative performance within the group), they are determined more by test difficulty than by anything else.

"Don't take 'Introductory' from Jones," I heard a student say the other day. "He doesn't know that the letter A exists." I have known such teachers; haven't you? Two teachers of the same subject may differ greatly in the number of As, Fs, etc., given to students of similar ability. Research shows that grading changes over time, too; average college grades today are higher than a generation ago.

No type of score is perfect. But Type I letter grades are worse than most others because they rely more on test difficulty than on true quality of performance (their apparent basis).

Compare with Type II B 3 letter grades.

TYPE II: INTER-INDIVIDUAL COMPARISONS

Type II scores are much more commonly used with standardized tests than with classroom tests. Almost all standardized tests use some version of Type II A, B, or D scores in their norms tables. Types II A and B may be used with typical-performance tests as well as with maximum-performance tests.

Type II scores are relatively independent of content difficulty, for they base an examinee's score on the performance of other people in a comparative (or *normative*) group. If the test content is inherently difficult, any specified person's raw score is likely to be lower than on an easier test; however, this difficulty of content will also influence the scores of the other examinees. Thus it is sometimes possible to use the same test for individuals (and for groups) ranging widely in level of ability. It also permits the test constructor to aim for test items of about 50 percent difficulty, the best difficulty level (from a measurement point of view) because it permits the largest number of inter-individual discriminations. On the other hand, all Type II scores are influenced by the level of the comparison group. For example, I will score higher when compared with college freshmen than when compared with college professors.

Type II A: Inter-Individual Comparison Considering Mean and Standard Deviation

In Type II A scores, we find that inter-individual comparison is expressed as the number of standard deviations between any specified score and the mean. As with all Type II scores, a change in norms group will influence the level of score.

Type II A scores are all *linear standard* scores. They are called *standard* because they are based on the standard deviation; we shall see shortly why they are *linear*. They may be viewed as statements of standard-deviation distance from the mean or as scores that have been given a substitute mean and standard deviation. All Type II A scores have properties which make them more valuable in research than most other derived scores: (1) for every test and group, each Type II A score gives the same mean and standard deviation; (2) these scores retain the shape of the raw-score distribution, changing only the metric or the calibration numbers; (3) they permit intergroup or intertest comparisons that are not possible with most other types of score; and (4) they can be treated mathematically (for example, averaged) in ways that some other scores cannot be.

1. z-score

The basic standard score is z. All other linear standard scores may be found directly from it. It tells in simple terms the difference (or distance) between a stated group's mean and any specified raw-score value.

Formula:

$$z = \frac{X - \overline{X}}{s}$$

where X = a specified raw score
$\overline{X}$ = mean raw score for some group
s = standard deviation of that same group

(Thus, if z-scores are found for each examinee in the group, the mean will be 0.00 and the standard deviation will be 1.00.)

Example: Willa White had a score of 49. She is to be compared with other local examinees; the mean and standard deviation of this group are 40 and 6, respectively. Willa's z-score = $(49 - 40)/6 = 9/6 = 1.5$. Willa's score is 1.5 standard deviations above the mean. (Assuming a normal distribution, we find that she did as well as or better than about 93 percent of this group.)

Although z-scores have distinct advantages for the research worker, they are not too handy for the test user, except as a step in computing other types of linear standard score. About one-half of all z-scores are negative, and all z-scores are expressed to one or two decimal positions. The other linear standard scores have been designed to eliminate the decimal point and obtain smaller units (by multiplying each z-score by a constant) and to eliminate the negative values (by adding a constant positive value to each score).

2. T-score

The T-score is one of the most common linear standard scores. Its rationale is the same as for the z-score, except that it has a mean of 50 and a standard deviation of 10.

Formula:

$$T = 10z + 50$$

where $z = \dfrac{X - \overline{X}}{s}$, as shown above

10 = a multiplying constant (that is, each z-score is multiplied by 10)

50 = an additive constant (that is, 50 is added to each value of $10z$)

Example: Willa White's z-score is 1.5; therefore, her *T*-score = 10(1.5) + 50 = 15 + 50 = 65. [Assuming a normal distribution, we find that she did as well as or better than about 93 percent of her comparison group. In any event (normal distribution or not), her *T*-score of 65 is directly under her z-score of 1.5 (see Chart 6.3).]

The *T*-score has much the same advantages and limitations as the z-score. It is somewhat less useful than z for certain research purposes, but it is more convenient to interpret since there are no negative values. (The probability of obtaining a value which is more than five standard deviations below the mean in a normal distribution is less than one three-millionth.) Nor do we typically use decimals with *T*-scores.

Unfortunately, *T*-scores are easily confused with certain other types of score, especially the *T*-scaled score (considered shortly as a Type II B score). These two *T*s are identical in a normal distribution, but may differ considerably in a badly skewed distribution. *T*-scores are often confused with percentile ranks, too, for they use similar numbers. The reader may wish to check these similarities and differences in Chart 6.3.

3. AGCT score

This score gets its name from the *Army General Classification Test*. It is similar to z and to *T*, except that it has a mean of 100 and a standard deviation of 20.

Formula:

$$AGCT = 20z + 100$$

> where z = a z-score, as defined above; and 20 and 100 are multiplying and additive constants, respectively

Example: Willa White's z-score was 1.5; therefore, her *AGCT* score = 20(1.5) + 100 = 30 + 100 = 130. [Assuming a normal distribution, we find that she did as well as or better than about 93 percent of her comparison group. In any event (normal distribution or not), her *AGCT* score of 130 is directly under her z-score of 1.5 and her *T*-score of 65 (see Chart 6.3).]

As originally used, the *AGCT* score was based on a large sample of soldiers who took the first military edition of the test; their mean was set at 100 and their standard deviation at 20. Subsequent editions of the test have been made to give comparable results. These scores are very similar to the deviation IQs that will be considered shortly; however, *AGCT*s have a standard deviation somewhat larger than commonly used with IQs. Although a convenient scale, *AGCT* scores are not in general use except in connection with the military and civilian editions of the *Army General Classification Test*.

4. CEEB score

This score was developed for the purpose of reporting the results of the College Entrance Examination Board tests and is used by the Educational Testing Service as the basis for reported scores on many of its other special-program tests (including the *Scholastic Aptitude Test, Graduate Record Examination,* and others). It is similar to other linear standard scores, but has a mean of 500 and a standard deviation of 100.

Formula:

$$CEEB = 100z + 500$$

where z = a z-score, as defined above

Example: Willa White's z-score of 1.5 would be expressed on this *CEEB* scale as 650. (Her percentile rank would be 93, assuming a normal distribution. In any distribution, her *CEEB* score of 650 lies directly under a z of 1.5, a T of 65, etc.)

As originally used, the *CEEB* scores were set up differently each year according to the mean and standard deviation of that year's examinees. They now are keyed to the mean and standard deviation of 1941 examinees, so that it is possible to compare results from one year to the next. Note, however, that because *CEEB* scores are not based on the present set of examinees, ETS also reports percentile ranks based on current examinees.

5. Deviation IQs (sometimes)

The IQ (Intelligence Quotient), suggested about seventy years ago by the German psychologist Stern, sounded very reasonable; Terman used it with the *Stanford-Binet* in 1916, and soon other test constructors began using it. Few tests still use the ratio IQ (a Type III score) where IQ is based on the ratio of mental age to chronological age. One big advantage of a deviation IQ is that it has a common standard deviation for all ages covered by the test on which it is determined.

The term *deviation IQ* is used to describe three different types of score. We shall deal here with the first meaning, a linear standard score [but see also Type II B 5(e) and Type IV C]. The deviation IQ has the same advantages and limitations as other linear standard scores except that it has a mean of 100 and a standard deviation as fixed by the test's author.

(*a*) *Wechsler IQs.* Three popular individual tests of intelligence are the *Wechsler Preschool and Primary Scale of Intelligence (WPPSI),* the *Wechsler Intelligence Scale for Children-Revised (WISC-R),* and the *Wechsler Adult Intelligence Scale-Revised (WAIS-R).* IQs are determined in somewhat similar fashion on all three—each test yielding a Verbal IQ, a Performance IQ, and a Full Scale IQ.

The author had decided in advance that he wanted his test to have a mean of 100 and a standard deviation of 15. He therefore used the formula: $IQ = 15z + 100$. The Wechsler user need only consult the appropriate tables to find the three IQ values.

(b) 1960 Stanford-Binet IQs. Until the 1960 revision, *Stanford-Binet (S-B)* IQs were ratio IQs. The authors of the 1960 revision decided to adopt the deviation IQ so that the standard deviation would be constant from age to age; in spite of careful and extensive effort in preparing the previous revision (1937), standard deviations for different ages had differed by as much as eight IQ points!

The *Stanford-Binet* has tasks arranged by age levels from two years to superior adult. Following carefully described procedures, the examiner finds a mental age from the test. This MA is entered into a table opposite the examinee's chronological age (an adjusted age, of course, for adults) and the IQ is found.

In the case of the *S-B*, we have a linear standard score with a mean of 100 and a standard deviation of 16. Separately for each chronological age group, the authors have used the formula $IQ = 16z + 100$. The metric employed is thus very similar to that used on the Wechsler tests, as may be seen in Figure 6.1 of Chart 6.3. (Note, however, that IQs found for the same examinee on the two tests might still differ; in addition to measurement errors, the tests also differ in content and in their norms groups.)

Summary of Linear Standard Scores

All linear standard scores tell us the location of an examinee's raw score in relation to the mean of some specified group and in terms of the group's standard deviation. In any distribution, normal or not, we can convert freely from raw-score values to linear standard-score equivalents without in any way changing the shape of the original distribution. Because of these properties, we can average these scores exactly as we can raw scores; *we cannot average other Type II scores.*

Type II B: Inter-Individual Comparison
Considering Rank

Like Type II A scores, Type II B scores are very commonly used in reporting standardized test results. Unlike Type II A scores, they are based on the number of people with scores higher (or lower) than a specified score value. Therefore, we lose such information as distance away from the mean. On the other hand, some of these scores (especially Type II B 5) have the effect of creating a distribution which is more nearly normal than the distribution of raw scores on which they are based. As with all other scores (except Type I), values will change for different comparison groups. Note: Because their units differ in size, Type II B scores should not be averaged.

1. Rank

The simplest possible statement of relative position is rank; first for highest or best, second for next, third for next, and so on. It has the unique disadvantage of being so completely limited by the number of cases that it is never used formally in reporting test results.

2. Percentile rank and percentile band

The percentile rank (sometimes called centile rank) is probably the score used most frequently in reporting the results of standardized tests. All things considered, it is probably the best type for general use in test interpretation; however, it does have limitations, as we shall see presently.

A percentile is any one of the 99 points dividing a frequency distribution into 100 groups of equal size. A percentile rank is a person's relative position within a specified group.

> We find the *percentile rank* of an examinee or of a given raw-score value. We find a specified *percentile value* by finding its equivalent raw-score value. Thus a raw score of 162 may have a percentile rank of 44; the forty-fourth percentile will be a raw score of 162.

Because of the importance of percentiles and percentile ranks, Charts 6.4(A) and 6.4(B) have been included to describe and illustrate their computation. The raw-score values used were selected deliberately not to conflict with the numbers used to express any of the more common derived scores. The range in raw scores is smaller and the number of people is smaller than we would expect to find for most groups; this was done deliberately in order to simplify the presentation.

TO FIND PRs FOR STATED RAW-SCORE VALUES

1. List every possible raw-score value.
2. Show the frequency with which each score occurs.
3. Find the cumulative frequency up through each score by adding that score's frequency to the frequencies of all lower scores; for example, *cf* through score of 214 (that is, through its upper limit, 214.5): $4 + 3 + 0 + 1 = 8$.
4. Find the cumulative frequency to midpoint of each score by adding one-half of frequency at that score to the cumulative frequency up through next lower score; for example, cf_{mp} for 212.0: $(\frac{1}{2} \times 0) + 1 = 1.0$; cf_{mp} for 216.0: $(\frac{1}{2} \times 4) + 12 = 14.0$.
5. Convert to cumulative percentage by the formula: $cP_{mp} = 100\,(cf_{mp})/N$, where cP_{mp} and cf_{mp} are defined as above, and N = number of cases; or, use $100/N$ as a constant to multiply by successive cf_{mp} values, as here: $100/N = 100/50 = 2.0$.
6. Find percentile ranks by rounding each cP_{mp} value to nearest whole number (except use $1-$ for 0 and $99+$ for 100).

CHART 6.4(A) *COMPUTATION OF PERCENTILES AND PERCENTILE RANKS*

1 X	2 f	3 cf	4 cf_{mp}	5 cP_{mp}	6 PR
225	1	50	49.5	99.0	99
224	1	49	48.5	97.0	97
223	2	48	47.0	94.0	94
222	4	46	44.0	88.0	88
221	2	42	41.0	82.0	82
220	5	40	37.5	75.0	75
219	6	35	32.0	64.0	64
218	8	29	25.0	50.0	50
217	5	21	18.5	37.0	37
216	4	16	14.0	28.0	28
215	4	12	10.0	20.0	20
214	4	8	6.0	12.0	12
213	3	4	2.5	5.0	5
212	0	1	1.0	2.0	2
211	1	1	0.5	1.0	1

where X = value of raw score

$\quad\quad f$ = frequency (number of examinees making this score)

$\quad\quad cf$ = cumulative frequency

$\quad\quad cf_{mp}$ = cf to midpoint of score

$\quad\quad cP_{mp}$ = cumulative percentage to midpoint of score

$\quad\quad PR$ = percentile rank for the specified raw-score value

TO FIND RAW-SCORE EQUIVALENTS OF PERCENTILE VALUES

1. Prepare columns 1-3 as in Chart 6.4(A).
2. Change from percentile to number of cases by multiplying P_x by $N/100$; for example, in finding P_{20}: $20 \times 50/100 = 10$.
3. Count up through the number of cases found in step 2, assuming that cases are distributed evenly across each score; for example, one-third of the cases at a score lie one-third of the way between the real lower limit and real upper limit of the score, one-quarter of the cases lie one-quarter of the way through the score, and so on. See the examples in Chart 6.4(B).
4. Corresponding raw-score value is the desired percentile.

Advantages and Limitations of Percentile Ranks. The principal advantage of PRs lies in their ease of interpretation. Even a person who thinks of

CHART 6.4(B)

EXAMPLES:
FIND P_{30}, THE RAW-SCORE VALUE AT OR BELOW WHICH FALL 30% OF THE CASES:

A. 30% of 50 cases = 30 × 50/100 = 15; we must count up through 15 cases.
B. Find the biggest number in the *cf* column that is *not greater than* 15. This number is 12.
C. Subtract the number found in step B from the number of cases needed; 15 − 12 = 3.
D. We need to get these three cases from those individuals at the next higher score; in other words, we need three of the four cases at the score of 216.
E. We go that fractional way through the score: ¾ (or 0.75) + 215.5 (real lower limit of score) = 216.25. P_{50} = 216.25.

FIND P_{50} (THE MEDIAN):

A. 50% of 50 cases is 25.
B. We note 25 in the cf_{mp} column; P_{50} = midpoint of the score, 218, or 218.0.

FIND P_{80}, THE EIGHTIETH PERCENTILE:

A. 80% of 50 cases is 40.
B. We note 40 in the *cf* column; P_{80} = upper limit of the score, 220, or 220.5.

We should note that in Chart 6.4(A) we have found cumulative frequencies up to the midpoint of each raw-score value, and have translated these cf_{mp} values into percentages which, rounded to whole numbers, are the percentile ranks.

percentiles as being equally spaced (which they could not be unless the same number of persons obtained each raw score) can understand something about these scores if he/she knows only that a PR is a statement of the percentage of cases (or persons) in a specified group who fall at or below a given score value.

On the other hand, we find it very easy to overemphasize differences near the median and to underemphasize differences near the extremes; in Figure 6.1 of Chart 6.3 we should note the slight difference between PRs of 45 and 55 as compared with PRs of 90 and 99. And even these varying differences are altered when a distribution departs markedly from the normal probability model, as may be seen in Figure 6.2.

Averaging Percentile Ranks. Because interpercentile distances are not equal, we cannot average them directly (as we could Type II A scores). This point applies equally against averaging the performance of one person on two or more tests and against averaging the performance of a group of people on one test.

To find the average PR of one person on several tests convert each PR to a z-score using the Conversion Table on page 152; average the z-scores; convert the average z to a PR. Note: This method assumes a normal distribution for each test and the same normative group for each test; only slight errors will be introduced if the distributions are nearly normal, but no averaging can be done if the PRs are based on basically different groups.

To find the average PR for a group of persons on one test, average the raw scores and find the PR corresponding to this average raw score. Note that this method is one we might follow to determine how our local group compares with a national normative group. Note further that this procedure gives the PR corresponding to the average raw score. Since group averages vary less than do individual raw scores, the value found should never be thought of as the PR of the group (in comparison to other groups). This misleading sort of information is contained in some test manuals.

More Advantages and Limitations. With percentiles, we are using a common scale of values for all distributions on all tests. Regardless of the range of raw scores, the range of PRs will be the same: 0 or 1 − to 100 or 99 + (unless more than 0.5 percent of the examinees make either the lowest possible score or the highest possible score). On very short tests, a difference of 20 or 30 PRs may represent a difference of only one or two raw-score values.

Some publishers use PRs of 0 and 100; some do not. The following example reflects the philosophical issue:

Lambert Lucas has a score lower than anyone in the normative group. A PR of 0 would certainly describe his performance. On the other hand, we like to think of a normative group as being a sample representative of a large population. If Lambert is being compared with an appropriate group, he presumably belongs to the population from which the normative group was taken. It is not logical to say that he did less well than everyone in the population of which he is part. Following this line of reasoning, I prefer to use 1 − instead of 0 and 99 + instead of 100.

Some readers may wonder how this issue can exist if a percentile rank, as defined a few pages back, is one of the 99 points which divide a frequency distribution into 100 groups of equal size.

Figure 6.3 gives us the answer. If we divide the ranked distribution of scores into 100 subgroups of equal size, as shown across the top of the line, there are 99 percentile points setting off the 100 subgroups. In expressing a percentile rank, however, we round to the nearest whole percentile value—as shown by lines drawn across the bottom of the line to indicate the real limits of each percentile rank. Ninety-nine of these units leave 0.5

percent at each extreme of the distribution: it is these extremes that we call
$1-$ and $99+$.

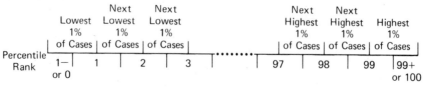

FIGURE 6.3.   Graphic explanation of percentile ranks at upper and lower extremes of a distribution. (See further explanation in text.)

One final disadvantage of percentile ranks is that they use a metric (or scale of numbers) that is shared with several other types of score: some examples are percentage-correct scores, *T*-scores, and IQs. There is the possibility of confusion, especially with percentage-correct scores. We must remember that percentage-correct scores are based on percentage of content (items), whereas PRs are based on percentage of cases (people) in a specific group.

Summary of Percentile Ranks

Although PRs have limitations, they are very commonly used in expressing the results of standardized tests. They are reasonably easy to understand and to explain to others. Considering all the advantages and limitations, PRs are probably the best single derived score for general use in expressing test results. Consider, too, the following application.

The percentile band

An interesting application of percentile ranks is found in the *percentile band* developed by the Education Testing Service and now used by several publishers. The percentile band is a band or range of percentile ranks. The upper limit of the ETS percentile bands corresponds to the percentile rank of a score one standard error of measurement above the obtained raw score; similarly, the lower limit is one standard error of measurement below the obtained score.

The width of the band may, of course, vary for different tests and different publishers; however, the general concept is the same. Publishers using the band approach give full information about it in their manuals. Test users wishing to make their own bands may do so—needing only a set of percentile norms, the standard error of measurement, and the directions above.

The purpose of percentile bands is to emphasize that test measurement error is present in each score. The percentile band is useful, too, in interpreting differences between different tests within the same test battery.

Percentile bands combine the stated advantages of the percentile rank with an emphasis that the score should not be treated as a precise value. In addition, it seems to have the advantages of other coarse-unit scores while avoiding their principal limitation (that a single unit of change is relatively large) by centering the band on the obtained score—thereby changing the limits of the band only slightly for slight differences in score. This may prove to be the most valuable single type of score for general test interpretation purposes.

3. Letter grades (sometimes)

As suggested earlier, letter grades may be based on comparative performance; when so used, they are a Type II B score. A few standardized tests have used such scores, each clearly indicating those values to be assigned As, those to be assigned Bs, and so on. Far more commonly, a teacher will use some inter-individual comparison in assigning course grades.

Note that it is not necessary to decide in advance how many students will receive each letter grade. "Grading on the curve" is rather old fashioned anyway. The practice of basing letter grades on a normal curve (perhaps by giving 10 percent A, 20 percent B, 40 percent C, 20 percent D, and 10 percent F) is indefensible unless one has very large numbers of unselected students. One way of assigning grades on the basis of comparative performance that I like is as follows:

> I make no assumption about the number of students who will fail or who will get any particular grade. During the term I give several quizzes and make certain that the standard deviation of each is about the same (for tests "weight" themselves according to size of standard deviation). I make the standard deviation of the final examination about twice that of one of the quizzes. I add these raw scores and arrange the students in order of summed scores. Often the results will show several clusters of students—suggesting that they be given the same grade. If there are students whose summed scores seem almost "to drop out" of the distribution, these may receive Fs. I will, however, consider carefully whether any of these students has shown a little promise—perhaps by great improvement on the final examination—that might justify some grade other than F. I try to be a little more generous with higher grades when my class has been better than usual. Some years my students seem less promising, and I am more cautious about assigning many high grades.
>
> I think that every teacher recognizes that grades are somewhat arbitrary and subjective. I try to make the grades I assign as fair as possible, reflecting comparative performance for the most part, but with just a dash of consideration for the sort of class I have.
>
> Let me know if you ever find the perfect grading system, will you?

4. Decile rank

The Institute for Personality and Ability Testing (IPAT) uses *decile scores* in some of its norms tables. A decile is defined as any one of nine points separating the frequency distribution into ten groups of equal size. Thus the first decile (D_1) equals the tenth percentile, the second decile (D_2) equals the twentieth percentile, and so on. R.B. Cattell modifies this meaning of decile to include a band (or range) of 10 percent of the cases—5 percent on each side of the actual decile point; for example, a decile score of 1 includes values from the fifth to fifteenth percentiles. (Values below P_5 are given a decile score of 0; values above P_{95}, a score of 10.) IPAT believes that these scores should be used in preference to percentile ranks when the range in raw scores is very small. In order to prevent confusion between decile and decile score (and to point out their similarity to percentile ranks), I prefer to use the term *decile ranks*.

5. *Normalized standard scores (area transformations)*

Normalized standard scores are derived scores that are assigned standard-score-like values but are computed more like percentile ranks. With *linear* standard scores, the shape of the distribution of raw scores is reproduced faithfully; if additional baselines were drawn for a frequency polygon, we would find that values of any of those standard scores would lie in a straight line below the corresponding raw-score values regardless of the shape of the raw-score distribution. With *normalized* standard scores this is true only when the raw-score distribution is normal—as shown in Figure 6.2 of Chart 6.3.

Normalized standard scores have the property of making a distribution a closer approximation of the normal probability distribution. This is accomplished in similar fashion for all normalized standard scores, so we consider the general procedure here rather than treating it separately for each score.

CHART 6.5   *HOW TO COMPUTE NORMALIZED STANDARD SCORES*

1. Find percentile rank for each raw score.
2. Use Conversion Table (pp. 152-57); find the percentile rank in the extreme right column; read the corresponding value from the appropriate column to the left.

Area transformations. As we can see from the computation procedures in Chart 6.5, these scores are known as area transformations because they are based on standard-score values that would correspond to specified cumulative percentages in a normal distribution (and area indicates frequency of cases).

To say that 23 percent of the cases lies below a specified score is the same as saying that the 23 percent of the area of a graph showing that distribution lies below that same score value. In finding a normalized standard score, we are merely substituting for that score value a standard-score value that would be at a point where 23 percent of the normal curve's area falls below.

(a) T-Scaled Score. In a normal distribution, this has exactly the same properties as the *T*-score (including its mean of 50 and standard deviation of 10). In fact, this score commonly is called *T*-score. It has all the advantages and limitations of the normalized standard scores already mentioned. It has the additional limitation of being confused with the *T*-score, which is of practical significance only when the distribution of raw scores deviates appreciably from the normal probability model.

(b) Stanine Score. Developed by World War II psychologists for use with the U.S. Air Force, stanine scores were intended to maximize the information about test performance that could be entered into a single column of an IBM punched card. Obviously a card could hold more one-digit scores than two- or three-digit scores. Whereas earlier standard scores had indicated specific values, stanines (from standard score of nine units) were intended to represent bands of values; except for the open-ended extreme stanines of 1 and 9, each stanine was to equal one-half standard deviation in width and the mean was to be the midpoint of the middle stanine, 5.

Apparently some Air Force psychologists used the stanine as a linear standard score at first, thereby giving it the properties mentioned above; however, others treated it as a normalized standard score, and it is so used today. When distributed normally, stanines have a mean of 5 and a standard deviation of 2; in addition, all stanines except 1 and 9 are exactly one-half standard deviation in width. With distributions which are not normal, these values will be only approximated.

In general, stanines have the advantages and limitations of other coarse-unit scores. It is unlikely that a person's obtained score is many units away from his true score, but a test interpreter is perhaps more likely to put undue confidence in the accuracy of the obtained score. For computation, see Chart 6.6.

Flanagan's Extended Stanine Score. For use in reporting scores on its *Flanagan Aptitude Classification Tests*, Science Research Associates splits each stanine value into three units by using plus and minus signs. Stanine 1 is made into three stanine values: $1-$, 1, and $1+$, and every other stanine is treated similarly. In this way John Flanagan achieves a 27-unit normalized standard score scale. His scale has certain obvious advantages over the usual stanine scale, but it is not in general use. The percentile equivalents of these extended stanine values differ slightly for each test in the *FACT* battery; they may be found in the *FACT Examiner's Manual*.

(c) C-Scaled Score. J.P. Guilford has developed a *C*-scale that provides one additional unit at each end of the stanine scale. The *C*-scale has eleven units assigned values of 0-10. This scale is used in the norms tables of tests

CHART 6.6   *HOW TO COMPUTE STANINES*

The purpose is to assign stanines according to the designated percentages; these are the normal-curve percentages that fall into each unit one-half standard deviation in width when we set up stanine 5 to extend from a z-score of -0.25 (one-fourth standard deviation below the mean) to a z-score of $+0.25$.

The ideal percentage is shown for each stanine on the top line below. The stanines to be assigned are shown in the bold face type. The bottom line shows the ideal cumulative percentages up through each stanine. We can only approximate these figures with real data—especially when either range or number of cases is small.

LOWEST	NEXT	NEXT	NEXT	MIDDLE	NEXT	NEXT	NEXT	HIGHEST
4%	7%	12%	17%	20%	17%	12%	7%	4%
Stanine **1**	Stanine **2**	Stanine **3**	Stanine **4**	Stanine **5**	Stanine **6**	Stanine **7**	Stanine **8**	Stanine **9**
4%	11%	23%	40%	60%	77%	89%	96%	100%

Cumulative Percentages

Steps in Computing Stanines
1. Draw up a frequency distribution.
2. Find the cumulative frequency up through each score value.
3. Change these cumulative frequencies to percentages by multiplying every *cf* value by 100/N.
4. Assign stanine values by approximating the *ideal* cumulative percentages on the bottom line above, as closely as possible.
5. Remember: each person with the same raw score must receive the same stanine score—regardless of how well each value "fits" the ideal percentages.

published by the Sheridan Psychological Services. *C*-scores are computed exactly as are stanines, except for the two extremes. See Chart 6.7.

Note that the *C*-values are identical with stanines except at the two extremes.

(d) Sten Score. Similar in rationale to the two preceding scores is the sten (a normalized standard score with ten units). This system provides for five normalized standard-score units on each side of the mean, each being one-half standard deviation in width except for the sten values of 1 and 10, which are open-ended. Since it is a normalized standard score, these interval sizes apply exactly only in a normal distribution. This metric is used for norms of some of the tests published by the Institute for Personality and Ability Testing. Stens may be computed in the same way as stanines, except that the values given are as shown in Chart 6.8:

CHART 6.7

LOWEST 1%	NEXT 3%	NEXT 7%	NEXT 12%	NEXT 17%	MIDDLE 20%	NEXT 17%	NEXT 12%	NEXT 7%	NEXT 3%	HIGHEST 1%
C = 0	C = 1	C = 2	C = 3	C = 4	C = 5	C = 6	C = 7	C = 8	C = 9	C = 10
1	4	11	23	40	60	77	89	96	99	100

Cumulative Percentages

CHART 6.8

LOWEST 2%	NEXT 5%	NEXT 9%	NEXT 15%	LOW MIDDLE 19%	HIGH MIDDLE 19%	NEXT 15%	NEXT 9%	NEXT 5%	HIGHEST 2%
Sten 1	Sten 2	Sten 3	Sten 4	Sten 5	Sten 6	Sten 7	Sten 8	Sten 9	Sten 10
2	7	16	31	50	69	84	93	98	100

Cumulative Percentages

(e) Deviation IQs (Sometimes). So far as I know, no intelligence test presently uses deviation IQ in this normalized standard-score sense, but such a use seems logical. Such deviation IQs would have the same general advantages and limitations as the *T*-scaled scores, except that their mean would be 100 and their standard deviation as determined by the author and publisher. In all other characteristics, they would resemble the deviation IQ (Type II A 5).

Wechsler subtests. Something similar to deviation IQs of the sort mentioned in the previous paragraph is already found in the subtests (or scales) of the Wechsler intelligence tests. Each of the separate scales on these tests uses a normalized standard score with a mean of 10 and a standard deviation of 3; however, these scale scores are used principally in finding total scores on which the Wechsler IQs [Type II A 5(a)] are based, and the subtest scores are seldom interpreted in themselves.

(f) ITED-score. The *ITED* score was developed for use with the *Iowa Tests of Educational Development*, but is now also used with the *American College Testing Program (ACTP)* and some other tests. This score has a mean of 15 and a standard deviation of 5 and is based on a nationally representative sample of tenth- and eleventh-grade students.

(g) Standard Age Score. Now used in connection with certain Houghton Mifflin tests (such as Thorndike and Hagen's *Cognitive Abilities Test*), the standard age score has a mean of 100 and a standard deviation of 16. Thus it has the same properties as the *Stanford-Binet* metric, except that the *SAS* is a *normalized* standard score.

(h) Normal Curve Equivalent (NCE). The *NCE* is a type of score developed by the RMC Research Corporation for use by the United States Office of Education. Its use is strongly recommended to educators and psychologists engaged in research projects for the USOE. It is *not* intended for interpretation of an individual's test results.

The *NCE* is a normalized standard score with a mean of 50 and a standard deviation of 21.06. *NCE* values can be found by calibrating the baseline of a normal curve from 1 to 99 in equal units—when 1 and 99 are made the equivalent of percentiles of 1 and 99. Thus, *NCE* values and percentile ranks are identical at 1, 50, and 99—as shown in Figure 6.4.

Type II C: Inter-Individual Comparison Considering Range

Only one derived score, the percent placement score, is based on inter-individual comparisons considering the range of raw scores. It is used in rare instances to express scores on classroom tests of achievement—and nowhere else.

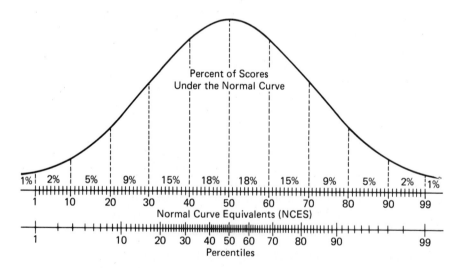

FIGURE 6.4. Relationship of NCEs and percentiles in a normal probability distribution. (Tallmadge and Wood, *User's Guide, ESEA Title I Evaluation and Reporting System.*)   The research worker probably will prefer to consult the conversion table in Tallmadge and Wood's *User's Guide, ESEA Title I Evaluation and Reporting System* from which Figure 6.4 was obtained.

Percent placement score

The *percent placement* score indicates a person's position on a 101-point scale where the highest score made is set at 100 and the lowest at 0.

Formula:

$$X_{\%\mathrm{pl}} = 100\,\frac{(X - L)}{(H - L)}$$

where X = any specified raw score
L = lowest raw score made
H = highest raw score made

Example: On a 300-item test, there is a range from 260 to 60; range = $H - L$ = 260 − 60 = 200. Barry's raw score was 60; the percent placement score is 0. Harry's raw score was 260; the $X_{\%\mathrm{pl}}$ = 100. Carry's raw score was 140; the $X_{\%\mathrm{pl}}$ = 40 [i.e., 100(140 − 60)/200 = 40].

Type II D: Inter-Individual Comparison Considering Status of Those Making Same Score

Type II D scores include *age scores* and *grade-placement scores*. These are set up to express test performance in terms of averages of groups which differ in status (either in chronological age or in grade placement). Thus the examinee's score is not a statement of how well one has done when compared with some single specified group, but rather a statement of that group (among several that differ in level) one is presumably most like.

Type II D scores are used most commonly with standardized tests of achievement and intelligence for children of school age. They are not suited for use with informal tests, and no computation guide will be given.

Although Type II D scores seem easy to understand, they have many limitations which are not immediately apparent.

1. Age scores

Age scores may be developed for any human characteristic that changes with age; however, they are used most frequently with intelligence and achievement tests for children of school age or below. The most common age score is the *mental age* (MA), a concept developed by Alfred Binet about 80 years ago for use with the earliest successful intelligence test.

An age score is an expression of an examinee's test performance stated in terms of the developmental level characteristic of the average child of that corresponding chronological age.

Karla gets an MA of seven years six months (expressed as 7-6) on an intelligence test. This means that Karla's level of performance is equal to the average score made by children with a chronological age of 7-6. Alternatively, although less frequently, an MA may be defined as the average chronological age of individuals making a given raw score. By this definition, Karla's MA of 7-6 would indicate that the average chronological age of children with the same raw score as hers was 7-6.

When used with young children, age scores are reasonably easy to understand. The logic is straightforward and simple. On the other hand, age scores are easily overinterpreted. A five-year-old who obtains an age score of 7 on a test is still only five years of age in most respects. There can be no assumption that all people with the same age score have identical abilities.

Test makers have difficulty in getting good representative samples for age norms because some children are located a grade or two ahead of (or behind) their age peers. These youngsters must be included if the norms are to be meaningful, but they are especially difficult to locate when they do not attend the same schools as their age peers. (See Type III scores.)

An age score by itself tells us little about the individual's potentiality, but it may be used in combination with chronological age or other measure to form a quotient score that will do so.

(a) Mental Age. Although the MA served Binet's need for a score that could be understood easily, it has been extended beyond reason. As originally conceived, MA units were credited to a child for each task that was passed. The sum of these units yielded an MA; this MA had the property of being equal *on the average* to chronological age.

On certain intelligence tests, however, MAs are determined by finding first the number of items correct. Then an MA is assigned according to the chronological age group for which that score is the average. When used in this manner, MA is merely an additional step in computing an intelligence quotient (IQ).

Still another unwarranted extension of the MA has been its application to adults. Although there is increasing evidence that at least some aspects of intelligence may continue to grow on into middle age, it is also true that the increment between successive ages becomes smaller with increasing age. There are more obvious mental differences between the ages of six and seven than between the ages of sixteen and seventeen or between the ages of twenty-six and twenty-seven. Even within the age range of five to fifteen, there is no basis for believing that MA units are equal in size. An age-scale approach is not feasible beyond the middle teen years, and, on tests where an age scale is used, all people beyond a given chronological age level are treated (in computing an IQ) as having the same chronological age. Any MAs reported as being above about sixteen or seventeen years are necessarily for the convenience of the test, rather than a reflection of the performance of people with those higher chronological ages. Some people, for example, will obtain scores which are higher than the mean for *any* age group. The nature of the mean guarantees this.

We must use considerable caution when interpreting MAs. Within the range of about five to fifteen years, MAs may be reasonably meaningful for children of approximately those same chronological ages; however, it is not correct to think of a mentally defective adult having, let us say, an MA of 6-0 as being equal to the average child of that age. The adult will have habits and motor skills differing greatly from those of the typical child, whereas the child will probably be able to grasp many new ideas much more readily than the retarded adult.

One difficulty with the interpretation of MAs is the fact that the standard deviations differ from test to test and even from age to age within the same test. Therefore there is no way of generalizing age-score values that are any stated distance from the mean; for example, an MA of 13-3 for a child of 12-3 does not indicate the same degree of superiority as does an MA of 6-3 for a child of 5-3.

(b) Educational Ages, etc. Very similar to the mental age is the educational age. An *educational age* (EA) indicates test performance at a given level—which level is expressed as the age of individuals for whom this is average performance.

> Krista Kitsinis has an EA of 8-6 on a test. In other words, her achievement on this test is equal to the average (mean or median) performance of children in the norm group who were eight years six months of age when tested; or, less frequently, this may mean that the average chronological age of children earning the same score she did is 8-6.

Actually, what we are calling simply educational age goes under many different names: *achievement age, reading age,* or *(any* subject matter) *age.* All the difficulties and limitations mentioned for the MA hold for the EA at least equally as well.

At some point the EA system must break down, for superior older children will earn scores which are above the average for *any* chronological age. EA values assigned at the upper limits must be arbitrary.

An assumption basic to the EA seems to be that children acquire knowledge and skill more or less uniformly throughout the calendar year—that is, that the child learns just as much per month during the long summer vacation.

2. Grade-placement scores

One score used very commonly in reporting performance of standardized achievement tests is the *grade-placement* (or *grade-equivalent*) score. Unfortunate! In spite of intrinsic appeal and apparent logic, these scores are confusing and lend themselves to erroneous interpretations.

The basic rationale of grade-placement scores is similar to that of age scores, for their values are set to equal the average score of school pupils at the corresponding grade placement. They are established by (1) testing youngsters at several grade placements with the same test; (2) finding the average (mean or median) for each grade-placement group; (3) plotting these averages on a graph and connecting these plots with as straight a line as possible; (4) extending (extrapolating) this line at both extremes to account for scores below and above the averages found; (5) reading off the closest grade-equivalent values for each raw-score value; and (6) publishing these equivalents in tabular form.

Grade-placement scores are usually stated in tenths of a school year; for example, 8.2 refers to the second month of grade eight. (This system gives a value of 1.0 to the beginning of the first grade—which presumably should be the true zero point in school grade placement.)

A basic assumption seems to be that children learn more or less uniformly throughout the school year (but that no learning occurs during the summer vacation).

Grade-placement scores are intrinsically appealing. It seems reasonable at first glance to think of children who stand high in comparison with others in their school grade as doing the same quality of work as youngsters more advanced in school. And in a sense they are. But that does not mean that these children should be promoted immediately to a higher grade. These grade-placement scores are based on the *average* performance of pupils having that actual placement in school. In obtaining that average, we had some better scores and some poorer scores.

Furthermore, regardless of how high a child's grade-placement score is, the child has had only a given amount of time in school. And there are probably breadths and depths of understanding and competency that are closely related to the experiences and to the length of one's exposure to school. A child's higher score is more likely to mean a more complete mastery of (and therefore fewer errors on) material taught at his/her grade. When this fact is considered, we see that the direct meaning of grade-placement scores is more apparent than real.

Grade-placement scores resulting from tests produced by different publishers are likely to give conflicting results. Not only is there the always-present possibility of their selecting different normative samples, but the tests of different publishers are likely to place slightly different emphases on the same subject matter at the same level. For example, among grammar tests, one test may include many more questions on adjectives than another test does. Such differences inevitably alter the grade-placement scores of individual pupils and of entire classes of pupils.

Standard deviations are bound to differ for various subject matters—even when the tests are included in the same standardized achievement test battery and based on the same normative groups. Students are much more likely, for example, to have grade-placement scores several grade equivalents higher than their actual grade placement in reading and in English than in arithmetic and in science. The latter subjects depend much more on specific, school-taught skills. The result is that standard deviations are almost certain to be larger for English and reading than for arithmetic and science; similar, less extreme, differences exist for other subjects.

Test manuals of all major publishers of achievement tests carefully point out these differences in standard deviations. Many test users, though, do not understand the critical importance of these differences in any interpretation of scores. Among many other points, these different standard deviations reflect the greater possible range in grade-placement scores on some tests of an achievement battery than on others. Grade-placement scores on one test may extend up 4.5 grade equivalents, as compared with only 2.5 grade equivalents for another test in the same coordinated achievement battery.

Grade-placement scores are so confusing that a lower score on one test may indicate relatively *higher* performance than does a higher score on another test. Because of the difference in size of standard deviations, the following might easily happen: a grade-placement score of 8.5 on reading may be equal to a percentile rank of 60, but a grade-placement score of 8.2 on arithmetic fundamentals may be equal to a percentile rank of 98. Especially for higher elementary grades and beyond, grade-placement scores cannot meaningfully be compared from test to test—even within the same battery!

The difficulties noted above are accentuated when we consider subtests based on very few items. Here the chance passing or chance failing of a single test item may make the difference of one full grade equivalent. *Who can get any meaning out of such a state of affairs?*

All of these limitations exist even when the test difficulty level is appropriate for the pupil. If the test is so easy that some pupils answer all questions correctly on any part, we cannot know the scores they could have made—they might have done much better if there had been more items of appropriate difficulty. Thus again the paradox: tests which are too easy for a pupil can give a score that is too *low*.

Test publishers know the limitations of grade-placement scores and point them out carefully in their manuals. But not all test users have a PhD in educational measurement. And the more carefully the publisher documents the limitations of each test and its score, the less likely is the typical user to read the manual carefully. Every major publisher includes at least some information about the equivalence of grade-placement scores to other types of score (percentiles, stanines, *T*-scores, and the like).

Test publishers have also been careful to point out that (1) grade-placement scores based on all pupils assigned to a given grade differ from those based on only those pupils whose actual grade placement is appropriate for their age (see "Modal-Age Grade-Placement Scores"), (2) grade-placement scores are not standards that should be obtained by all pupils as a prerequisite for promotion, and (3) separate tables are needed when comparing average grade-placement scores for different classes or schools (because averages vary less than do individual scores).

Yet these mistaken beliefs persist.

(a) Full-Population Grade-Placement Scores. Many sets of grade-placement norms are based on all of the pupils in those classrooms used in developing the norms. This practice has been found to produce rather large standard deviations of grade-placement scores and to make the raw score corresponding to a given grade-placement score seem rather low. When all pupils are included in the normative samples, there is a fair percentage of children included who are overage for their actual grade placement (because of nonpromotion or illness), and a few who are underage for their actual grade placement.

(b) Modal-Age Grade-Placement Scores. The presence of overage and underage pupils in classes used for normative purposes is thought to be undesirable. Most publishers now use modal-age grade-placement scores either exclusively or in addition to the full-population norms.

Modal-age indicates that only those pupils who are of about average age for their grade placement are used. The practices of publishers differ somewhat, but their aims are similar. One publisher may include all pupils who are not more than one year underage or overage for their grade placement; a second publisher may use only those pupils within three months of the modal chronological age for a specified grade placement.

Modal-age norms are a little more select. When both full-population and modal-age grade-placement norms are compared, we find that higher raw scores usually are needed to attain a given grade-placement score on modal-age norms.

(c) Modal-Age and Modal-Intelligence Grade-Placement Scores. A further refinement of grade-placement scores is the practice of basing the norms only on pupils who are of near-average intelligence as well as being near-average in chronological age for actual grade placement. This should not have any pronounced effect on grade-placement values, but some believe the practice provides a better guarantee of a grade-placement score that is truly representative of average performance.

In developing these age- and intelligence-controlled score values, the California Test Bureau used only pupils with IQs of 98–102, who were within three months of average age for their actual grade placement (for grades one–eight). Progressively higher IQs were used for successively higher grades.

TYPE III: INTRA-INDIVIDUAL COMPARISON

All Type III scores are unique in that they are based on two measurements of the same person; all are found as ratios or fractions.

Type III A: Ratio IQ (Intelligence Quotient)

Although we have considered the IQ twice before and will return to it once again (under Type IV), this is the original IQ—the one first proposed by Wilhelm Stern and first used by Lewis Terman in 1916. The *ratio-type intelligence quotient* is found by the formula: IQ $= 100 \ MA/CA$, where MA is a mental age found from an intelligence test, and CA is the examinee's chronological age at the time of testing (with an adjusted CA used for older adolescents and adults). It is rarely used today.

The rationale of the ratio-type IQ is widely understood, but its many limitations are less well known. The score depends on an assumption of equal-sized mental-age units which may not exist. Ratio-type IQs work reasonably well between the ages of about five to fifteen years, but tend to be of questionable value outside those approximate limits. Adult IQs of necessity are based on artificial mental ages (as explained earlier) as well as "adjusted" chronological ages.

The most telling argument against the ratio IQ, however, is that standard deviations differ from one age level to the next. If standard deviations are permitted to vary (and this cannot be controlled with a ratio IQ), the same IQ indicates different degrees of superiority or inferiority at different ages. The deviation IQ (Type II A or II B) is much better than the ratio IQ.

Type III B: Intellectual Status Index

A concept introduced by the California Test Bureau for use with its *California Test of Mental Maturity* is the *Intellectual Status Index*. This is a sort of IQ substitute with the denominator changed from a child's actual chronological age to the average chronological age of children with his same grade placement in school.

The score is based on the premise that a pupil's score on an intelligence test is determined more by his placement in school than by his chronological age. The logic sounds reasonable, but the user should check carefully the size of standard deviation at different age levels. We must be careful, too, not to confuse *ISI* with *IQ*, especially for children who are either overage or underage in their respective grades.

Type III C: Educational Quotients

An *Educational Quotient* is found by dividing an educational age (EA) by chronological age (CA) and multiplying by 100. Just as we may have subject-matter ages of all sorts, so may we have all sorts of subject-matter quotients. EQs have never been very widely used, for grade-placement scores have been preferred.

Type III D: Accomplishment Quotients

There is almost unanimous agreement that the *Accomplishment* (or *Achievement*) *Quotient* (*AQ*) is a poor type of score. Not only is it based on two test scores, each with its own errors of measurement, but it also gives illogical results. It compares a pupil's achievement test score with an intelligence test score, and it is presumed to indicate how completely one is working up to capacity.

Formula:

$$AQ = 100 \frac{EA}{MA}$$

where EA = educational age, determined by an achievement test
MA = mental age, determined by an intelligence test

The ideal AQ is 100, indicating that a pupil is realizing complete potential. How, then, do we explain an AQ above 100? Although logically impossible, AQs above 100 can occur—suggesting that some pupils are achieving better than they are capable of achieving! A much more reasonable explanation, of course, is that the two scores entering into the AQ are fallible measures and that errors of measurement have combined to produce this "impossible" result.

TYPE IV: ASSORTED ARBITRARY BASES

Although the three main bases for expressing test scores are sufficient to account for most commonly used scores, there are still more bases that are unique. We shall mention three very briefly.

Type IV A: Nonmeaningful Scaled Scores

Several publishers use scaled scores that are nonmeaningful in themselves but which are extremely useful in giving a common basis for equating different forms and/or levels of a test. The previously mentioned CEEB score, as used today, has many elements of such a scaled score. CEEB scores originally were linear standard scores with a mean of 500 and a standard deviation of 100; however, now the results of each year's edition are keyed statistically to the 1941 results. Thus, these CEEB scores are not directly interpretable for today's examinees, and percentile ranks are used for that purpose.

We shall consider only one more example: the *SCAT* scale developed by the Educational Testing Service. This is a nonmeaningful scaled score used with its *School and College Abilities Tests (SCAT)* and its *Sequential Tests of*

Educational Progress (STEP). ETS deliberately sought a scale using numbers that would not be confused with scores from other scales. The scale was constructed so that a scaled score of 300 would equal a percentage-correct score of 60; and a scaled score of 260, a percentage-correct score of 20. These scaled score values are used as a statistical convenience for the publisher, but percentile bands are used for interpreting results.

Type IV B: Long-Range Equi-Unit Scales

None of the scores already mentioned has a scale of equal units except within a narrow range or under certain assumptions. For some purposes, it is most desirable to have a single equi-unit scale covering a wide span of ages.

An early attempt at constructing such a scale resulted in the *T*-score mentioned earlier. As originally conceived by W.A. McCall, this scale was to use 50 for the mean of an unselected group of twelve-year-olds. The mean for older groups would be higher, for younger groups lower. The standard deviation would be 10 at all age levels.

Another early attempt was made by Heinis, who developed mental growth units that he believed were more nearly uniform in size than mental age units. These, in turn, were made to yield a Personal Constant, which he felt was more consistent than the IQ over a period of years. Although Kuhlmann-Anderson norms have used the PC, they have never been widely accepted.

One more example of such a scale is the *K*-score scales developed by Gardner. The average score of tenth-graders is set at 100, and the unit of measurement is set at one-seventh the standard deviation of fifth-graders. The rationale underlying the scale is too technical to go into here, but it has been applied to the *Stanford Achievement Tests* (published by Harcourt Brace Jovanovich). The principal advantage of such long-range equi-unit scales is to be found in various research applications. For the most part, they do not lend themselves well to direct interpretation. Their underlying rationale is usually very involved and their development complicated. The reader who is interested in such scores may obtain further information from any of the more technical measurements references.

Type IV C: Deviation IQ (Otis-Style)

It is fitting, perhaps, to come to the end of our long succession of scores with another IQ—the fourth one we have mentioned. (Is it any wonder that the IQ is a confusing score?)

The deviation IQ as used on earlier Otis intelligence tests and certain others is basically different from the Type II deviation IQs. In the development of the Otis-style deviation IQ, a norm (or average) is found for each age group. We obtain an examinee's IQ by finding the raw score, subtracting the age norm, and adding 100; the result shows deviations of examinees from their age norms in raw-score units.

Formula:

$$\text{(Otis) IQ} = 100 + (X - \overline{X}_{\text{age norm}})$$

where
X = any person's raw score on an Otis intelligence test
$\overline{X}_{\text{age norm}}$ = average raw score for those in norm group whose chronological age is same as examinee's

This deviation IQ has a mean of 100, but the standard deviation is not controlled as were the standard deviations of the Type II deviation IQs. Because of this, the standard deviations of Otis-style IQs may vary from age to age and make interpretations difficult. Note: The newer *Otis-Lennon Mental Ability Test* (The Psychological Corporation) uses a Type II A 5(a) score, the Wechsler-type of deviation IQ.

A FINAL WORD

We have considered many types of test score in this chapter. The personnel worker in industry is likely to encounter relatively few of them—probably only Types II A and II B (inter-individual comparisons considering mean and standard deviation, and considering rank within group). The school teacher or the guidance worker may very well encounter almost any of them.

Test scores would be much easier to interpret—for all of us, experts and novices alike—if only we could agree upon a single type of score or even on just a few.

Considering all factors, I should like to see the day when we would use only percentile ranks or percentile bands in test interpretation. This score has limitations, to be sure, as all scores do. But the score has some inherent meaning and is easy for the layman to grasp. With a single type of score, we could direct our attention to educating everyone to its meaning and to its principal limitation, the difference in distances between various percentile points. We could stress, too, the importance of knowing the composition of the norm group (or groups).

There is little question but that percentile ranks can do everything that the IQ can. Percentile ranks within grade or within age have many advantages over grade-placement and age scores.

We might still have need for special warning about the use of percentile ranks on very short tests where the difference of a single raw-score value may mean a great difference in percentile rank, but the percentile band, of course, is a protection here. We still have need for other kinds of scores for research, because percentile ranks do not lend themselves well to mathematical manipulation; indeed, we cannot even average them.

We must remember that a test score must be understood before it can be interpreted. It would be easier to learn one score thoroughly than to try to learn something about many assorted scores.

Even more significant than any of these considerations is, of course, the quality of the test itself. A good test is one that will do the job we want it to, will do so consistently, and will possess those practical features (such as cost, time required, and the like) which make it usable for our purposes.

7 | TEST PROFILES

A test profile is a graph that shows the test scores of one individual (or, less often, of average scores for a classroom or other group). Until recently, most profiles were drawn locally, usually by a teacher, personnel worker, or clerk. More often today we see profiles that have been computer-produced.

Local preparation has obvious advantages where few examinees are involved or where a unique set of tests makes up the test battery administered. If an agency has norms of its own that are based on the same group of people, it is permissible to use a common profile form for reporting results from different tests. We should use separate forms whenever we have different norms groups.

Figure 7.1 shows a computer-prepared profile for the *Differential Aptitude Tests*. These results are for Pat Paraskevopoulos who was tested in the fall semester of the ninth grade. The profile proper shows percentile bands for each of the tests in the battery; these bands are similar to score Type II B 2, but they are wider. On the profile, each band is designed to differ significantly from all other tests whose bands do not overlap; that is, the difference between the two tests is sufficiently great that the likelihood of the difference being due solely to chance is less than 5 percent.

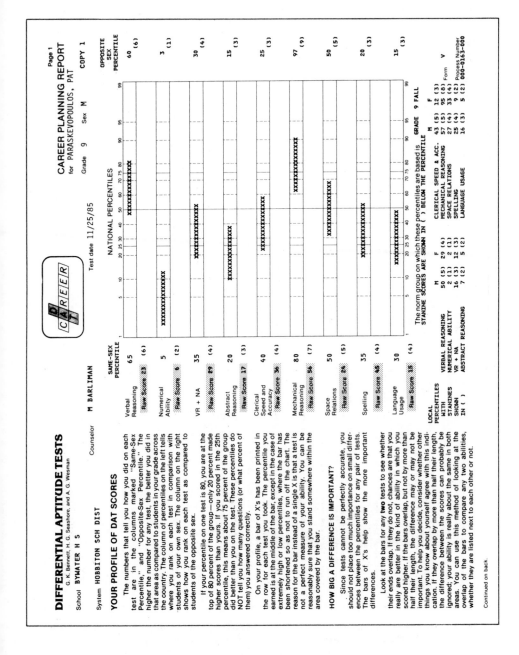

FIG. 7.1 Reproduced by permission from the Differential Aptitude Tests. Copyright © 1982, 1973, 1972 by The Psychological Corporation, New York, N.Y. All Rights Reserved.

Page 2

CAREER PLANNING REPORT

for PARASKEVOPOULIS, PAT

The report printed below is based on your answers to the *Career Planning Questionnaire* and on your aptitudes as measured by the *Differential Aptitude Tests*. Remember that this report tells you how things look at the present time, and that your interests and goals may change. To help you in understanding the report, descriptions of the tests are printed on the reverse side of this form, followed by the groups of school subjects and activities, and the groups of jobs and occupations.

In your Career Planning Questionnaire you indicated that you are 15 years old, a male in the 9th grade, and that you expect to graduate from high school and go to a technical, trade, or business school. Furthermore, you said your grades put you in the lowest quarter of your class. Among the groups of school subjects and activities, you said you like the following: Crafts; Technical Subjects; School Maintenance.

You indicated that your first choice of career goals was in the group called: Crafts & Trades. This field of work is related to the school subjects and activities that you like. It also matches your educational plans and your pattern of aptitude test scores. It appears that this field is a good career choice in terms of your interests, abilities, and educational plans.

You indicated that your second choice of career goals was in the group called: Engineering & Applied Science. People who choose this kind of work usually like the school subjects and activities you like. However, they typically get more education than you are planning to get. Also, their scores on some of the related aptitude tests are generally higher than yours. To sum things up, you should probably reconsider this occupational choice and think about other careers that are more suited to your educational plans and abilities.

You indicated that your third choice of career goals was in the group called: Farming & Conservation. The statement printed above for your first choice is appropriate for this choice, too.

Other occupational areas that match your abilities and school subject preferences:

    Medically Related*

    Business—Sales & Promotion*

    Visual & Performing Arts

* Requires more education than you are currently planning; you may wish to review your educational plans.

Any lack of agreement of your present occupational goals with the kinds of school subjects and activities you like, or with your tested aptitudes, suggests that you might reconsider your career plans. The *Occupational Outlook Handbook* (published by the U.S. Department of Labor, and available in most public and school libraries), your school counselor, your parents, and other interested and informed adults may be useful sources of information and helpful to you in making decisions about what to try out and what to aim for.

DATA SERVICES DIVISION
THE PSYCHOLOGICAL CORPORATION
HARCOURT BRACE JOVANOVICH, PUBLISHERS

Separate at this fold

FIG. 7.2   Reproduced by permission from the Differential Aptitude Tests. Copyright © 1982, 1973, 1972 by The Psychological Corporation, New York, N.Y. All Rights Reserved.

Although only same-sex percentile bands are shown graphically, the form shows raw scores, same-sex and opposite-sex percentile ranks and stanines (national norms), and same-sex and opposite-sex percentile ranks and stanines (local norms). Additional valuable information about the meaning of the profile is printed at the left of the form. Even so, good testing procedure advocates the oral interpretation of results by a trained counselor.

Figure 7.2 compares Pat's test scores with his responses to the *Career Planning Questionnaire*. The *CPQ*, taken at the same time as the tests, asked him questions about such things as his occupational interests and his educational plans. The program tests the compatability of his statements and his *DAT* scores.

Figures 7.3 and 7.4 illustrate a somewhat different approach to profiles. They show the two sides of the Pupil Profile Chart and Individual Cumulative Record for the *Iowa Tests of Basic Skills*. One side (Figure 7.3) has spaces for recording the scores of a pupil on all of the tests in the battery for as many as ten test administrations. Figure 7.4 enables the school to draw profiles on the same form for those same ten testings. The metric shown along the ordinate of the profile is the Grade Equivalent score (Type II D 2)—multiplied by 10 to remove the decimal point (for example, a grade-placement value of 6.3 is shown as 63).

Another use of a profile is illustrated by Figure 7.5. This is the Tardor Report of Individual Test and is used for summarizing the results of a testing with the *Wechsler Adult Intelligence Scale-Revised*. The form is an aid for the clinician who wants to see a sort of summary of the performance of an examinee. Nancy Namyl, the hypothetical examinee in Figure 7.5, shows a considerable range in her ability on subtests of the *WAIS-R*. This form would call the examiner's attention to those subtests that may have clinical significance because they are either especially high or especially low. It is not a necessary tool for any psychologist experienced with the test, but it can help to direct attention to important aspects of the test performance.

General Profiles

It was formerly common practice to list and graph all tests taken by an individual on a single form. The careful counselor would note the different norms groups that were involved. Nevertheless, it was very easy to neglect the gross differences in the different groups. I strongly recommend using separate profile sheets for each of the tests given—unless, of course, it can be shown that the norms groups are comparable. (Note again, what a difference different norms can make.) See page 73.

The Good Profile

What is a good profile? The examinee's name, of course, must appear—together with any other identifying information such as date of

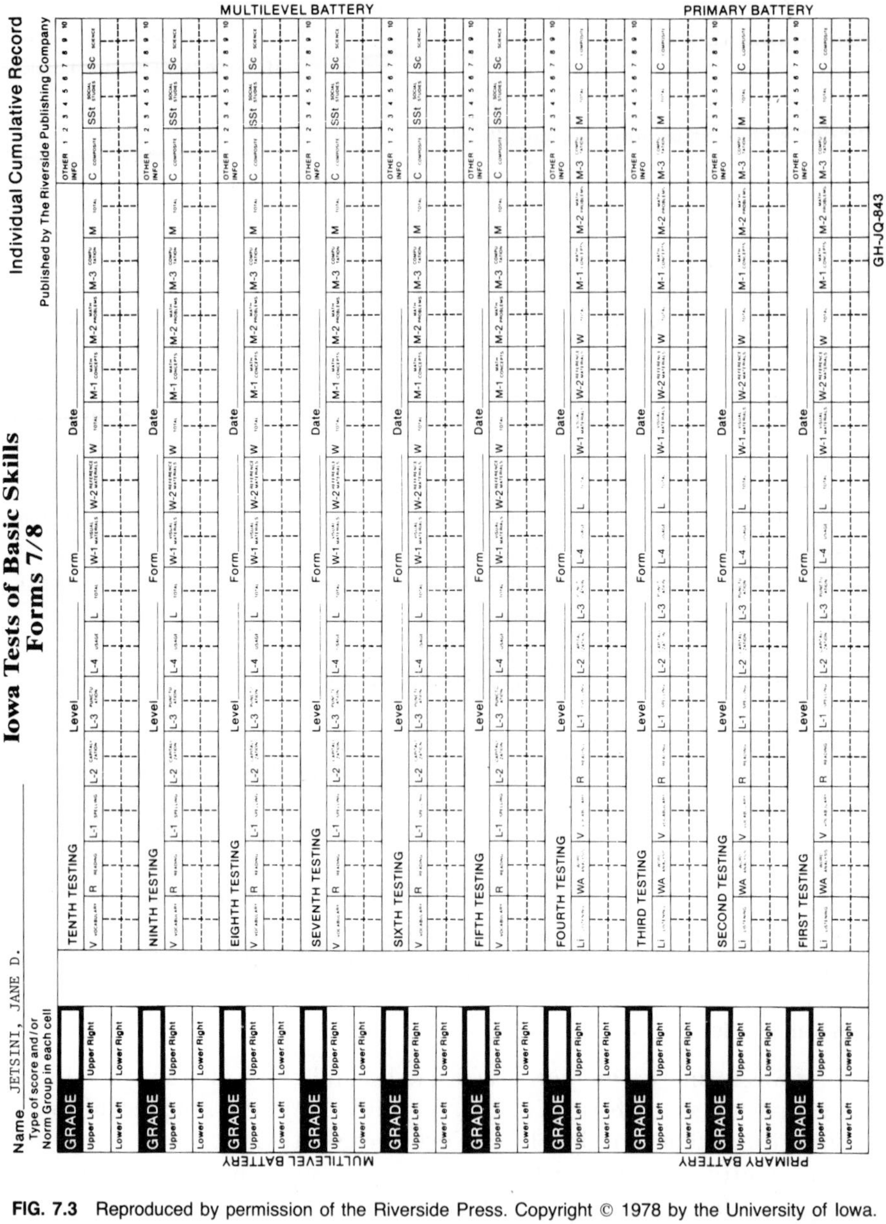

FIG. 7.3 Reproduced by permission of the Riverside Press. Copyright © 1978 by the University of Iowa.

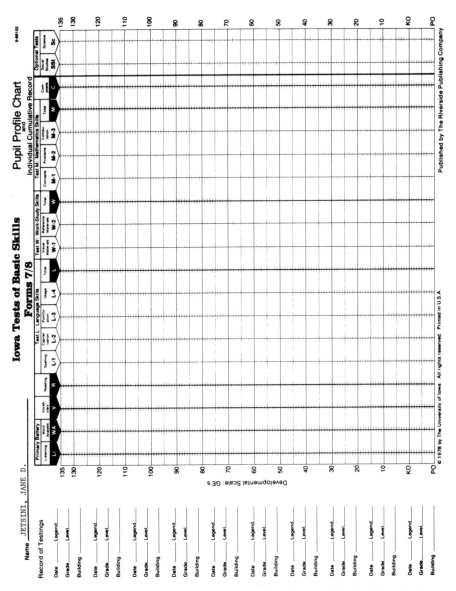

FIG. 7.4 Reproduced by permission of the Riverside Press. Copyright © 1978 by the University of Iowa.

─── REPORT OF INDIVIDUAL TESTING ───

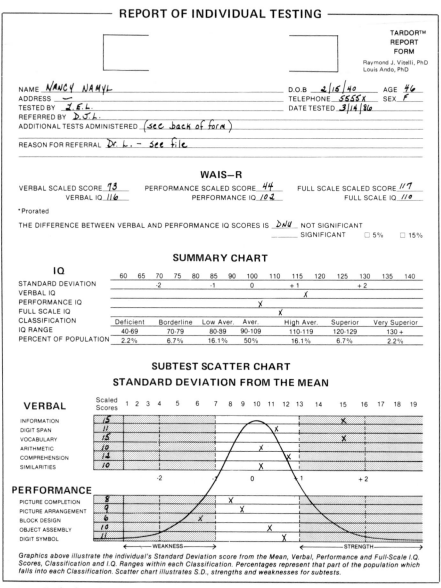

TARDOR™
REPORT
FORM

Raymond J. Vitelli, PhD
Louis Ando, PhD

NAME *NANCY NAMYL*   D.O.B *2/15/40*   AGE *46*
ADDRESS   *—*   TELEPHONE *5555X*   SEX *F*
TESTED BY *I.E.L.*   DATE TESTED *3/14/86*
REFERRED BY *D.J.L.*
ADDITIONAL TESTS ADMINISTERED *(see back of form)*

REASON FOR REFERRAL *Dr. L. – see file*

WAIS–R

VERBAL SCALED SCORE *73*   PERFORMANCE SCALED SCORE *44*   FULL SCALE SCALED SCORE *117*
    VERBAL IQ *116*   PERFORMANCE IQ *102*   FULL SCALE IQ *110*

*Prorated

THE DIFFERENCE BETWEEN VERBAL AND PERFORMANCE IQ SCORES IS *DNU* NOT SIGNIFICANT
    SIGNIFICANT   ☐ 5%   ☐ 15%

SUMMARY CHART

IQ	60	65	70	75	80	85	90	100	110	115	120	125	130	135	140
STANDARD DEVIATION			-2			-1		0		+1			+2		
VERBAL IQ										X					
PERFORMANCE IQ								X							
FULL SCALE IQ									X						
CLASSIFICATION	Deficient		Borderline		Low Aver.		Aver.		High Aver.		Superior		Very Superior		
IQ RANGE	40-69		70-79		80-89		90-109		110-119		120-129		130 +		
PERCENT OF POPULATION	2.2%		6.7%		16.1%		50%		16.1%		6.7%		2.2%		

SUBTEST SCATTER CHART
STANDARD DEVIATION FROM THE MEAN

VERBAL	Scaled Scores	1	2	3	4	5	6	7	8	9	10	11	12	13	14	15	16	17	18	19
INFORMATION	15															X				
DIGIT SPAN	11											X								
VOCABULARY	15															X				
ARITHMETIC	10										X									
COMPREHENSION	12												X							
SIMILARITIES	10										X									

                               -2   0   +1   +2

PERFORMANCE																				
PICTURE COMPLETION	8							X												
PICTURE ARRANGEMENT	9								X											
BLOCK DESIGN	6					X														
OBJECT ASSEMBLY	10										X									
DIGIT SYMBOL	11											X								

←———— WEAKNESS ————→   ←———— STRENGTH ————→

Graphics above illustrate the individual's Standard Deviation score from the Mean, Verbal, Performance and Full-Scale I.Q. Scores, Classification and I.Q. Ranges within each Classification. Percentages represent that part of the population which falls into each Classification. Scatter chart illustrates S.D., strengths and weaknesses for subtests.

FIG. 7.5 Tardor Report of Individual Test.

birth, grade and school, company and department, and so on. The examiner's name can be important when an individual test has been given. The date or dates of testing should be indicated. A note should be attached indicating any deviation from standard testing procedure that may have occurred. There must be no ambiguity as to the nature of the norms group.

A clear and precise description of the types of score used should be included, preferably on the form itself. If profiles are to be prepared locally, the publisher should provide clear directions for their preparation.

Regardless of the metric used in the profile, raw scores should also be reported. If scoring and profiling are done locally, the cautious user may want to check all of the scoring.

> I recently participated in a doctoral oral examination. The candidate, as part of her research, had examined several hundred *WAIS-R* protocols. She decided to check the arithmetic on each form before going further with her study—and found mistakes in arithmetic, usually small, on fully 25 percent of the forms. One should be compulsive with scoring tests that are to be used in practical settings!

Significant Differences in Profile Points

In interpreting test scores from profiles, one must be careful not to overinterpret apparent differences. We need specifically to consider the standard error of measurement. The difference between test scores may not be so great as it looks!

If the norms are not the same for two tests, there is no way to tell whether the scores are truly different. Nor can we tell unless tests use the same metric. We can't, for example, compare an IQ with a percentile rank.

Every test score includes some amount of error. If one were to take a large number of comparable forms of the same test, the scores would vary somewhat from form to form even if the forms were designed to give identical results on the average. As noted in Chapter 4, the standard error of measurement is an estimate of what the standard deviation of a person's scores would be if one were to take these many forms.

When two tests are involved, both scores are subject to measurement error, and we must consider both standard errors. We can be very certain that a given difference is a real difference (one that is not caused solely by the unreliability of the tests) if bands extending out two standard errors of measurement from each score do not overlap; however, this is a more rigorous standard than we need to use. We can estimate the standard error of difference in scores through the use of the formula

$$SE_{\text{diff meas}} = \sqrt{SE^2_{\text{meas}\,x} + SE^2_{\text{meas}\,y}}$$

where
$$SE_{\text{meas}\,x} = \text{standard error of measurement on Test } X$$
$$SE_{\text{meas}\,y} = \text{standard error of measurement on Test } Y$$

There are more technically sophisticated formulas that may be used when a substantial correlation exists between the tests. These may be found in any psychometrics text.

Profile Analysis

Whenever there are several scores reported for an individual (as in a profile), one may be tempted to try a profile analysis—that is, to try to find additional meaning through a study of the relative peaks and dips in score. On the *Wechsler Adult Intelligence Scale-Revised*, for example, some clinical psychologists believe that relationships between scores on certain of the eleven subtests can be used as a basis for personality diagnosis; however, except when the differences are very large, there is little clear-cut evidence that such diagnoses are meaningful.

Hundreds of studies involving profile analysis of the *Minnesota Multiphasic Personality Inventory* have been published, and some of them seem very rewarding. Similarly, Gough proposes interpretations for various combinations of scores on his *California Psychological Inventory* (Consulting Psychologists Press).

The meaningfulness of any sort of profile analysis depends in part upon the reliability of the tests that enter into the analysis and the reliability of the differences in score. No difference can have psychological or educational significance unless the difference is sufficiently large to be considered *statistically* significant (probably due to something other than pure chance).

There are many circumstances where scores may be used jointly to obtain better prediction of criterion values than can be obtained through the use of any one variable by itself; however, this topic (multiple correlation and multiple regression) is beyond the scope of this book.

8 | COMMON SENSE

When test results do not make sense, the test results may be wrong—or our "common sense" may be faulty. Neither is perfect.

Any testing program should call for checking at every stage where mistakes are possible. As test users, we should be prepared to check the scores that are put into our hands. If the test results do not seem reasonable, they *may* be wrong:

> Years ago I was looking over a multiple-score test taken by a college student as part of a campus-wide testing program. I was surprised that this good student had no scores above the median. Upon checking, I discovered that one of the scoring clerks had not understood the directions for using the norms table. She had taken raw-score values from the test, entered these in the percentile-ranks column, and read out the corresponding entries in the raw-score column as percentile ranks. Since there had been no systematic checking of results, more than 1,000 test sheets and profiles had to be re-examined.

Even today, with computer-scoring common, mistakes can occur. And, of course, the expectations may have been in error, and the tests may be right:

> A company was testing several people for a junior-level management position. Al Athol had been an employee of the company for several years, had a

good work history, and was well liked by fellow employees and by management. The other candidates were very recent college graduates and new to the firm. Al did as well as the other candidates except on a spatial relations test; on this, he did very poorly. The personnel director decided to select one of the other men because of this one very low score—and it is doubtful whether spatial relations skill was even involved in the management position! This personnel director should have used common sense, for Al was clearly superior to the other men on the various nontest factors that should have been considered.

In this following situation, common sense prevailed:

Cathie Cudder had worked in the divisional offices of Bigchain Grocery for nearly ten years. Her job required little typing and no shorthand, but did keep her in telephone contact with all stores within the division. When the divisional vice president fired his secretary, none of the more than eighty secretaries in the office dared to apply for the vacancy; they were afraid of the "VP." Ms. Cudder wasn't afraid, but the personnel manager wouldn't recommend her for the position because her secretarial speeds were below those required. Cathie called the vice president and requested an interview. Despite her slowness on typing and shorthand tests, she got the position because the vice president noted her strengths: (1) she was not afraid of him; (2) she knew company policy; and (3) she knew every store manager, assistant manager, and head cashier in the division. She could reacquire the secretarial skills. She worked successfully with him until his retirement four years later.

When test results and common sense seem to be in conflict, we need to check all possibilities: (1) tests may be wrong; (2) common sense may be wrong; (3) both may be wrong; and (4) neither may be wrong.

Let us see how common sense can be wrong. Are we sure that our preconceptions are correct? Is this really an able person or has the person succeeded by saying the right thing at the right time? Is this student really good or merely an "apple polisher"? Are these tests as valid for our purpose as they should be? What makes these test results seem unreasonable?

Often we find that questioning the results will help us to find errors in both our reasoning and the results. In such situations, checking really pays off, for it enables us to obtain a better understanding of the entire situation.

What about those situations, though, where test results seem unreasonable, and yet both our reasoning and the test results seem correct even after checking? In such situations we should probably stop to consider whether there is really a discrepancy between the two. Closer scrutiny may prove that the tests are giving us just a slightly different slant than the one we had been considering. Or perhaps the discrepancy is not so great as we had thought at first. If these lines of reasoning fail to resolve the discrepancy, we may want to get further information from other tests, interviews, and so on, provided that the situation is important enough to justify the effort.

Decision Making

Test scores often are used as one basis for making decisions. Tests are especially helpful when used in connection with institutional decisions about personnel, for in these cases there is a backlog of information from similar situations in the past, and the expectation is that many similar decisions will have to be made in the future. The institution is not likely to be hurt badly by a few bad decisions about the selection or rejection or classification of any individual. And tests, in their place, can provide information that may increase the accuracy of prediction in the long run. Common examples include the selection of students or employees and the classification of personnel.

Individual decisions, on the other hand, cannot be evaluated in the long run. Any specified individual is not likely to have to make this same sort of decision again. And the choice that individuals make right now may very well have a long-lasting effect on their respective lives. Test information, although sometimes helpful, can nowhere be *so* helpful as in institutional decisions. These individual decisions are important and unique to the person. The individual has no backlog of similar situations—nor the expectation of facing similar situations in the future. Common examples include such decisions as which curriculum to study, whether to attend college, which college to attend, and which job to take.

We can see why tests are better at helping us to make institutional decisions than at making individual decisions. Even with the best of tests, we expect to make some mistakes; however, if we have reasonably valid tests, we can make better personnel decisions with them than we can without them.

In contrast are the guidance and counseling situations in which tests may be used. If tests are considered in making individual decisions, we must be very cautious. Except in extreme cases, no test can tell, for example, whether a student should go to college or which type of training one should take. Often tests can be of most help in a negative way; that is, by ruling out certain alternatives.

Some Common Mistakes

Besides the measurement error inherent in any test, there are many possibilities of mistakes being made in the administration and scoring of a test and in reporting its results. The test user should make it part of the regular routine to check reported test scores whenever feasible.

Some sort of check should be made at every stage of testing to insure near-perfect accuracy of conditions for administration, scoring, and recording. Most of the mistakes are relatively simple things: failing to start the stopwatch used in timing; failing to wind the stopwatch; failing to stop at the proper time limit; omitting part of the directions; using the wrong answer sheet; using the wrong scoring key; lining up the scoring key incorrectly; making a mistake in counting; using a wrong scoring formula; using the wrong norms tables; reading the norms table incorrectly; misreading a handwritten score; making an error in copying, and so on. Over the years I have discovered some classic mistakes. I shall pass a few of them along, partly for comic relief and partly to show that one cannot be too compulsive in checking on tests.

> One national testing program once sent me a set of the wrong tests. The tests were not to be opened until the morning of the examination, and when they were—did we have fun!
>
> I shall never forget the chaos created when about 500 of 1,200 machine-scoring answer sheets proved to have been printed a little off center—not enough for the eye to notice, but more than enough to throw the scoring machine off. Hand-scoring a sample of answer sheets showed that something was wrong, but it took us several days to find the cause.
>
> I once received three successive orders of a standardized test which was printed just a bit too small; unfortunately, the scoring key was of standard size and did not match.
>
> Errors in the scoring keys of standardized tests are rare today, for they are very carefully checked; however, errors have been known to crop up even here. There is even the story (true, I think) of several people who managed to steal a preliminary scoring key of an important test they were to take; they were caught and found guilty when they turned in perfect papers—except for the three items which had been incorrectly marked on that preliminary key.

And, of course, I have made a few mistakes myself.

It is human to err, we are told. Most of these mistakes, though, could have been prevented.

Other Sources, Too!

Tests are only one source of information. And test scores are only bits of information. In any important decision, we should make full use of all of the information available to us. As information collectors, tests do have certain advantages—most especially their objectivity. But tests are fallible instruments, and test scores are fallible bits of information.

If tests are to be used, they should contribute something. People managed to exist and to make decisions without the aid of tests for many years—and they can today. If tests provide helpful information, we should use them—if they do not, we should not! And even when we do use tests, let us not forget to consider nontest factors as well—they, too, can be important.

We cannot repeat too many times that the message is even stronger for those using tests in industrial or personnel settings. There *must* be evidence of the validity of the test (or other procedure) if it is used for the selection or rejection of people for employment.

9 || WHAT CAN WE SAY?

We have been concerned primarily with the task of helping test users to understand the meaning of test scores. This may be sufficient for many test users, but certainly not for all.

School counselors, guidance workers, and many others have the additional responsibility for communicating test results to all sorts of other persons. This is more involved and requires additional skill. While this task is not our main concern, it is not one that we can ignore.

No amount of reading, or course, is going to make us expert at interpreting test scores. Written admonitions are no substitute for personal experience. Even so, it is possible to learn some general principles and "tricks of the trade." Our primary emphasis in this book is directed at enabling people with limited backgrounds in psychological and educational testing to understand the nature of test scores. There is no suggestion that this book can substitute for a basic course in tests and measurements or for a course in counseling or guidance techniques. These and other courses are needed *along with practice* before a person is prepared to get full meaning from test data.

There are two main topics in this chapter: (1) Who is entitled to test information? and (2) What do we say?

WHO IS ENTITLED TO TEST INFORMATION?

As a starting point, the examinee is entitled to receive information about test results. Federal law now underscores that right.

The Examinee

Information given to the examinee should be as detailed as is warranted by the test and as detailed as he/she is likely to understand. Specific scores should be given only when the examinee is also given a thorough explanation of what the scores mean and what their limitations are.

The legal requirement that schools must make test results available upon request imposes an additional professional responsibility. School personnel have an obligation to ensure that all results released are accompanied by meaningful interpretation!

Except within the clinical-counseling or court-legal frameworks, examinees should be told the results of the tests in as much detail as they are likely to understand; however, information should not be forced onto those who cannot assimilate it. This incident, for example, never should have happened:

> Bobby, a third grader, was skipping down the corridor at school and chanting, "I'm a genius! I'm a genius!" Bobby did not know what the word meant, but he did know that it must be something good because his parents had been so pleased when ". . . a lady came to our house and gave me a test. And then she said, 'Why, he's a little genius!' "

Parents of Minors

In the case of minors, parents must also be told the test results if they make such a request—as is provided in the Buckley Amendment (Federal Family Educational Rights and Privacy Act of 1974).

Agency Policy

School and other agencies are likely to have their own policies regarding the interpretation of test results. These policies should be made known to all people within the agency who have access to test scores, including secretaries, file clerks, and receptionists. As a rule, only professional-level workers should interpret scores to examinees, parents, or other laymen; however, in a well-run agency, there may be provisions for routine release of scores to specified professional people under stated conditions. (By *professional* in this chapter, I mean to include teachers, personnel workers, and others whose positions involve working with people, but to exclude general office workers.)

Schools and Colleges

With schools and colleges, routine test results should be handled in the same way as grades and personnel files. In the event of transfer to another institution or system, these routine test results should be sent along. It is imperative that furnished test information include date of testing, names of tests (with form, level, and edition), and raw scores; if derived scores are included, the norm groups should be identified.

On the other hand, tests given for counseling purposes (especially at the college level) should *not* be transferred automatically. This is testing that has been done for the student's personal benefit, and test scores should not be transmitted without the written permission of the student or (if under 18) of parents.

Professional Colleagues

Within any given agency (including a school system), any professional worker who has need for test data should have access to the scores. If there is reason to believe that the data are being misused, the access should be denied or withdrawn.

> Merry Melody, a music teacher, used to come to the counseling office toward the end of each semester and request intelligence test scores of her pupils. After a semester or two, it was noted that she was using these scores as a basis for assigning her course grades. The director of counseling spoke to her about the inadvisability of this practice. When, after two subsequent sessions, she still used the scores in this fashion, she was refused further access to the test scores.

When professional workers outside the given agency request test data on a person, it should be cleared through channels. These channels should include a release (in writing) from the examinee or the parents. Scores should not be released to nonprofessionals outside the agency.

Personnel

Certain differences may be noted in the handling of test data in personnel settings. Although the company or agency may employ the psychologist or the personnel specialist, it seems clear that the applicants or employees may demand to see their own test results. At least in certain types of setting (for example, civil service), examinees must be shown their test papers and a copy of the test.

The American Psychological Association's Division of Industrial-Organizational Psychology[1] recommends that reports to management not

[1]APA Division 14, *Principles for the Validation and Use of Personnel Selection Procedures,* 1975.

include specific scores, but only an interpretation of the results. They further recommend that employee files be purged every few years so that obsolete data do not introduce bias into employee matters. Personally, while recognizing the sincerity of their interest, I disagree with this latter point—believing (perhaps naïvely) that the data can be used as evidence of employee growth and for research purposes.

Test data should not be released to anyone outside the company except with the written permission of the individual.

In Conversation

We do not discuss, either publicly or in casual conversation, the test results of any of our examinees. It is permissible, or course, to identify the individual and test scores in a case conference in either a school, personnel, or clinical setting. But we cannot ethically continue our discussion of the individual outside the conference room!

COMMUNICATING THE RESULTS

The two essential steps in test interpretation are (1) understanding the test results and (2) communicating these results orally or in writing to another appropriate individual. And, in all instances, remember to get the examinee's permission in writing.

To a Trained Professional Worker

When the other person is trained in testing, the task of communicating results is relatively simple. We may start by giving the test name (including form, level, and edition—if pertinent) and the raw scores. We may include derived scores, if desired, along with the norms group(s) used. If both of us know our tests, there is every reason to believe that the information will be communicated accurately. If the information is communicated orally, we may take a few shortcuts; however, if the report is made in writing it should be complete.

When making a written report to another professional worker in whom I have confidence, I find the following method both convenient and economical:

> I include a Xerox copy of test profiles and the like. To this, I add a short letter of transmittal pointing out any unusual aspects of the case (either about the person or the test results); I also note irregularities (if any) in the testing procedures. If the examinee has been in counseling with me, I may include on a separate sheet a brief summary of our contacts to date, together with my observations about probable major problem areas and my expectation of

outcome. I address this material to the professional worker personally and mark it "CONFIDENTIAL."

The availability of copying machines is a tremendous boon to those who handle tests, for there is no danger of mistakes when making copies in this fashion.

Whenever there is the slightest doubt about the testing knowledge of the person to whom we send test scores, we should add some further explanation of the tests and the scores.

> "The *NEW Test* is a new scholastic aptitude test put out by the PDQ Company; we have been trying it out this year to see how well it compares with the *OLD Test*. The norms groups seem to be reasonably comparable, and we have found that our students tend to do about the same on both tests; however, the *NEW* is a little more highly speeded, and some of our teachers do not like it so well for that reason. You will note, too, that the publisher's national norms are given in stanines. I do not know whether you have been using stanines at your school, so I have included approximate percentile values for each one. Please let me know if I can be of further help. . . ."

The aim of test interpretation is, after all, to insure that the other person understands the results of testing. We do not fulfill that purpose unless we take all reasonable steps to state the results meaningfully.

To a Professional Worker Untrained in Testing

When test data are being given to a professional worker who is relatively untrained in testing, it is advisable to give both a written report and an oral interpretation. Unquestionably some of the best work of this sort is done by school psychologists in their reports to school principals and teachers. By and large, school psychologists do a remarkably good job of working with individual children and of reporting their findings. They seem much more interested in delivering informative and helpful reports than in showing off their erudition through overuse of technical jargon.

Reports to school teachers, to members of management, to personnel workers, to academic deans, and to others who typically have limited training in testing should be drawn up very carefully. We cannot assume that they know the difference between percentage-correct scores and percentile ranks; they probably do not. We cannot assume that they know what a standard score is—or an IQ—or an age score. Our reports need to be informative.

> "Betty's PR on the *Otis* is 74," is a statement that does not mean much to a person who does not know that PR means *percentile rank*, does not know what percentile rank means, and does not know what the *Otis* is. (And this particular statement would be only a little more meaningful to those of us who do

understand these points, for there still are several *Otis* tests in use and many different norms groups.)

This form would be much more helpful:

"On the *Blank Aptitude Test*, Betty did as well as or better than 74 percent of the recent applicants for clerical positions with our company. We find that about 60 percent of the women with similar scores have obtained at least Satisfactory ratings after six months on the job . . ."

Or, perhaps, this:

"On the *Blank Aptitude Test*, Betty did as well as or better than 74 percent of the students entering our college this past September. This score suggests that she should be capable of doing the work required in her program."

To a Mature Examinee

Trained and experienced counselors will have developed skills and techniques of their own, and new counselors should be developing them through specialized training and in-service supervision. We are concerned with techniques that can be used effectively and safely by relatively untrained test users.

Individuals suspected of severe maladjustment should be referred to specialists wherever possible. Our examinees are presumed to be adolescents or adults who have no disabling problems.

The following list of suggestions is not exhaustive. I think that most of them would be accepted by nearly all experienced test users:

1. Test interpretation usually is done within some greater purposeful situation: Examples include counseling, guidance, placement, and selection. There are times, however, when the test interpretation itself is sufficient reason for the interview—especially with high school students.

2. Look over the test results before the interpretation interview. Make sure that you understand them and have some idea of what you want to say.

3. Establish a comfortable working relationship with the examinee and make certain that you maintain interest and attention.

4. Be careful of your words. Examinees can be depended upon to remember your careless remarks and to misunderstand what they do not want to hear. Your care can keep distortion to a minimum.

5. Explain something about every test variable you interpret. The examinee may know nothing about the various types of test and probably knows nothing about the specific tests taken.

6. Explain the nature of the norms groups being used, especially when they differ for the various tests.

7. Sometimes, especially in a counseling setting, an opening like this is helpful: "How do you think you did? Do you have any idea which tests you did best on?"

8. If you feel comfortable in doing so, show the examinee the profile sheet(s); use this (them) as your basis for interpretation.

9. Do not force the interpretation on the examinee. You are wasting time. Point out that you may be available later, but that you feel it is pointless to continue under such circumstances. (I can think of some exceptions, but not many; the point is that, desirable though it might be for the examinee to know the test results, one is unlikely to understand them under stress.)

10. Interpret all of the test variables, not just those on which the examinee has done a good job. One has a right to learn both personal limitations and personal strengths. (Even a trained counselor, though, may prefer not to interpret some personality test variables.)

11. It is more difficult to interpret low scores than high ones. Designations of high and low are somewhat arbitrary, but not entirely so (see the suggestions at the end of this chapter).

12. Low scores are more easily accepted if they are stated in objective terms, such as: "Of people with scores like yours, only 10 percent have managed to maintain a passing average and to graduate in that curriculum" (see expectancy tables, pages 57-59).

13. Sometimes low scores may be made easier to accept when the nature of the test is *slightly* distorted. I sometimes point out to a student who has done poorly on an intelligence or scholastic aptitude test: "This means that you are very low in book-learning ability when compared with other high school juniors nationally. A few students with scores like yours may succeed in college through very efficient planning and extra-hard studying, but your high school grades suggest that you have not been achieving well in actual class situations, either."

14. Sometimes low scores can be communicated successfully through an analogous statement: "Mr. Dean, director of admission at Ourstate University is like anyone else. He likes to bet on the winners. He knows that students with better high school grades and higher test scores than yours are more likely to do well in college. Like a gambler, he will sometimes play a long shot and will be delighted when one pays off. But, for the most part, he has to select those people who seem most likely to succeed."

15. Never make a direct prediction, such as: "This score means that you will never make it to college," or "This test score proves that you would never succeed on this job," or "With scores like these, you are a cinch to get through college with flying colors." You can be very, very wrong! You are much safer to talk in group terms, such as: "Very few students with such scores . . ." or "Most students with scores such as these are able to do well in college if they study reasonably hard."

16. Do not assume that your examinee will remember everything. Try to help the person remember the important elements by summarizing the results; perhaps something like this: "In general, then, you show average or better ability to learn, and you show near-average achievement in most areas. But you seem to be somewhat lower in dealing with abstract or mathematical reasoning."

17. If appropriate, make general suggestions: "Our company likes to promote only people who have higher scores on tests of verbal ability. Have you considered going to night school? You could pick up an English course or two that might be helpful—and our company policy is to pay at least part of the expense." Or, perhaps: "Your scores suggest that you may have difficulty in getting into medical school. On the other hand, you do have good grades here

in high school—and this is important. You might be wise to select a small liberal arts college where you can hope for more individual attention and try for high grades in premedical work. Perhaps you will make it. Just to be on the safe side, though, you may want to consider some possible alternatives if you do not make med school. Sometimes people find it very difficult if they have given no thought to other things and then have to change plans at the last minute." Or, perhaps: "You have scores very high on the various English tests. Have you ever thought of working on the school paper? You might find it very rewarding."

18. Do not forget: The examinee decides what will be done. As a test interpreter, you may make suggestions but not decisions. (As an academic dean, placement director, and the like, you may make institutional decisions; the examinee makes individual decisions.)

19. Test interpretation often provides a good way of opening a discussion of the examinee's problems, plans for the future, and so on. If you are not a trained counselor, decide in advance how far you can go in receiving the examinee's confidences.

20. Don't interpret an examinee's scores solely in writing. Supplementary interpretation, especially through interpretive folders, may be very helpful. Most counselors feel strongly, however, that we should not rely exclusively on written interpretations because they provide no opportunity for counselee feedback.

21. Most important of all: Know what you are doing, do what seems natural and effective to you, and try to be genuinely helpful to the examinee.

To a Child

Some teachers try to explain achievement test results to elementary school children, especially when using the results in deciding to which areas the pupils may need to give special attention. Other than this, little effort is made to interpret tests to children who are below high school age.

I think that this reluctance is unfortunate. Children have considerable capacity for understanding, and they have tremendous curiosity. Some people may disagree, but I believe that some basic interpretation can be done effectively with children as young as ten years of age. The teacher may discuss the general nature of the tests with the class as a group. This can be followed up by an individual conference with each pupil, perhaps focusing attention mainly on areas of highest and lowest achievement and a statement about achievement relative to ability (without saying much about the intelligence level itself). Such interpretations need to be handled carefully, but can help youngsters in their search for an understanding of themselves.

Even with children of junior and senior high school age, most test interpretation should be couched in general terms. Children like to see things in clear-cut terms and are likely to oversimplify or overgeneralize. They are not likely to remember the test limitations so well as they remember specific facts that are mentioned casually or incidentally.

Superior students can handle somewhat more detailed interpretations. The interpretation can perhaps be used as an opportunity for emphasizing the importance of acquiring good study habits and developing a sound background for future work.

Special care must be used when interpreting results to children of below-average ability in order not to discourage them from trying to do their best. In dealing with this problem, the skilled counselor should be able to help the older child come to an acceptance of his limitations and to an appreciation of what can reasonably be accomplished through sustained effort. There is little kindness in encouraging unrealistic ambitions in the below-average child, but it is cruel to make the child feel worthless and stupid. There is evidence, too, that children tend to grow up to our expectations—so it may be advisable to overaccentuate the positive.

Encouragement can be especially helpful to the young child. Perhaps a set of low scores can be explained, "You may have to study harder and longer than some boys and girls do to get good grades." There is ample evidence that young children can respond positively to encouragement.

> One of my graduate students recently reported the following incident to me. Her son, Tommy, came home and said that he had gotten an A on a standardized achievement test battery. Tommy's second-grade teacher, it developed, had announced aloud in class letter-grade equivalents (including Fs) for the test performance of every pupil. Such letter grades exist only in the teacher's mind—they are not given in the manual!
>
> This incident, of course, is an example of bad interpretation. No second-grader is likely to learn much from such a procedure, and with few exceptions (such as a scholarship competition) public announcement of test scores is grossly unethical—and most sadistic!

To Parents

Very much the same considerations involved when interpreting test scores to mature examinees are involved when interpreting scores to parents. Parents, though, are more likely to be argumentative and to question the accuracy of the test results. Parents of children with low test scores are likely to be very defensive, and special caution must be used to make the parents view the results as objectively as possible. They must not be allowed to develop hostility toward the child because "he's so dumb," nor should they be given encouragement that "she's just passing through a phase."

Parents of a child of superior intellect may question why Paul is not doing better work and getting better grades if he is so intelligent. They may also question whether the school is doing its part in challenging the child to do his best work. (Consider carefully whether some such criticism may not be justified. Is the school doing what it can to meet the needs of the superior youngster?)

Parents differ markedly in their ability to understand and accept test results. I have no hesitancy in discussing actual scores (IQs, percentile ranks, or whatever) with some mature parents. Others, defensive from the start, make me shudder even at the thought of giving any sort of interpretation! Be careful! And try to know beforehand how detailed an interpretation you will give.

Also: remember the Buckley Amendment! The law says that you *must* make those data available to parents.

High and Low

How high is high? Your answer is probably as good as anyone else's. Except for a few considerations, it is an arbitrary decision.

First, we need to remember that scores are never completely accurate. Therefore, we should never say that any score is high unless it is at least one or two standard errors of measurement above the mean; otherwise, the above-average score may differ from the mean only by chance. The same line of reasoning, of course, operates in calling scores low.

Second, we must remember the way in which scores tend to cluster about the mean in typical distributions of test scores. The distance between successive percentile values is very small near the middle of the distribution. Thus, a given difference in percentile ranks reflects only a slight change in raw scores near the average but a large change in raw scores near the extremes.

Third, we have to remember that scores used in reporting standardized tests are relative rather than absolute. A given raw score may place an examinee high when compared with one group, but low when compared with another group.

Fourth, because of the greater reliability (and relatively smaller standard errors of measurement) of some tests, we may have more confidence in our use of high and low with such tests than with other, less reliable, tests.

I generally use something like the following descriptive scale:

PERCENTILE RANKS	DESCRIPTIVE TERMS
95 or above	Very high; superior
85-95	High; excellent
75-85	Above average; good
25-75	About average; satisfactory or fair
15-25	Below average; fair or slightly weak
5-15	Low; weak
5 or below	Very low; very weak

This is not an inflexible standard, but I find it a helpful one. Sometimes we vary these designations, or apply more (or less) rigorous standards.

If a graduate engineer were being compared on company norms with general clerical employees (perhaps the only norms the company has for the test), we might regard a percentile rank of 88 as being only "satisfactory" or "reasonably good."

In the same way, a graduate student who scores near the eightieth percentile on national undergraduate norms is probably only "about average."

IN SUMMARY

1. The person who interprets test results, however casually, must understand the nature of the tests and of the test scores. If you don't understand them yourself, you should not try to explain them to others.
2. Examinees and/or parents are entitled to an interpretation of all tests taken, and in as much detail as can be understood.
3. Test interpreters should try to avoid hurting people. Whenever possible, they should aim at giving some sort of realistic encouragement to examinees.

10 || TESTING AND SOCIAL RESPONSIBILITY

Testing is in an *era of schizophrenia*, according to some authorities. By this, they are referring to the fact that attacks on testing are becoming ever more virulent—at the same time, there is ever-increasing demand for tests and testing.

Few people under the age of seventy have not been exposed to some sort of standardized test. School children often take standardized achievement test batteries and may take intelligence and aptitude tests as well. Many school systems use vocational interest tests as part of their guidance programs.

College-hopefuls usually take either the *SAT (Scholastic Aptitude Test)* or the *ACT (American College Testing Program)*. Applicants for graduate or professional schools may expect to take such a test as the *Graduate Record Examination,* the *Miller Analogies Test,* or the *Law School Admission Test.* Additional tests are used for admission to such specialized practices as psychology, law, medicine, and dentistry.

Noncollege-bound youth are likely to encounter tests for admission to apprenticeship training, for gaining employment, for promotion on the job, and the like. Others face tests in military service or in civil service. And many people take still more tests in connection with counseling or psychotherapy.

In all sorts of ways, tests occupy a prominent place in our lives. I believe that it is important for those of us who work with tests to strive for them to be used responsibly. Often I start a course in Psychological Testing by asserting:

1. **Some tests are sometimes good in some situations.**
2. **Not all tests are always good in all situations.**
3. **Our task is to determine which tests are good in which situations.**

We use tests when there is reason to believe that we can use the results to help ourselves or others to make decisions more efficiently. We do not give tests solely for the sake of giving tests.

Despite the increasing use of tests and the increasing applications of testing, the value of testing has been under attack since the 1960s. Standardized tests have been accused of several shortcomings:

- not measuring innate (that is, inborn) intelligence
- being unfair to minorities
- not measuring creativity
- labeling children as morons, dopes, slow learners, and so on
- favoring the glib individual and penalizing the thoughtful person
- invading privacy
- giving inconsistent results
- being grossly misinterpreted
- *et cetera, et cetera, et cetera*

Some critics have been responsible in their concerns over widespread test usage. Others have seemed more concerned with selling a magazine article or a book. Even senators and congressmen at federal and state levels have entered the battle over the use of tests.

How can we explain the increased use of tests in view of all of these criticisms?

Part of the explanation may be that there has been a slight change in the emphasis of tests. It seems likely that there is slightly less intelligence testing going on, but that there has been an increase in aptitude and (especially) achievement testing. Aptitude batteries (such as the *Differential Aptitude Tests*) are tending to replace intelligence tests.

The increase in achievement testing has been phenomenal. Not only is there a steady demand for the norms-referenced achievement batteries, but there has been the development of criterion- or objectives-referenced testing throughout the past decade. Additionally, there have been numerous local scandals as high school graduates in various states have been found lacking in seemingly basic skills.

This latter situation has resulted in increased demands for proficiency tests to demonstrate that schools develop minimum skills in students before graduating them. Most states now have some sort of statewide assessment program.

Many of the adverse comments are true—or partly so. Much of the legislative attention has been a sincere effort to guarantee that tests are used responsibly—and I believe that they will have a long-term beneficial influence on testing. There still is a great need to educate people in the *responsible and intelligent use of tests*. Tests can be helpful in many situations, but they are not the complete and ultimate answer to every problem.

One big difficulty that most critics tend to ignore is this: the elimination of testing would solve very little. One cannot legitimately evaluate tests against a criterion of perfection; sometimes the absence of tests has disadvantages of another sort.

My answers to the series of charges against testing? You have already heard my views (in Chapter 1) on a couple of these issues, but let me explain in greater detail.

Tests do not measure innate ability

Of course they don't. Or, they don't measure *only* innate ability; they measure a great deal more: any ability test (aptitude, intelligence, or achievement) always measures some combination of innate ability, the influence of environment, and one's motivation at the time of testing (and perhaps other factors as well).

> I was giving a short series of lectures on testing to a class of first-year psychiatric residents. These are people who have an MD degree and are now starting their training to become psychiatrists. In this particular group were several foreign-born physicians who had been in this country for only a brief period of time. I was illustrating the administration of one of the most popular individual tests of intelligence. As I went around the table asking sample questions of each one, I received failures on these (simulated) items: "In what direction would I be going if I traveled from Detroit to Dallas?", "What is a 'civil rights' law?", and "What does the word 'collect' mean?" The questions were asked respectively of an Iraqi, a Greek, and a Brazilian. I had little difficulty in making this class appreciate that tests are necessarily at least partially culture-bound!

Rather obviously, people who have survived the educational system—in the United States or elsewhere—for long enough to obtain a medical degree are clearly above average in intelligence . . . regardless of their performance on specific items of this (or any) intelligence test.

> The professional literature on the relative importance of genetic and cultural bases of intelligence fills many volumes. The controversy is sometimes very bitter, and I shall not perpetuate it here; however, the accuracy of work of one eminent hereditarian, the late British psychologist Sir Cyril Burt, is now seriously questioned.

I believe that both heredity and environment are important—both in the determination of intelligence test scores and in the determination of a person's effective intelligence. Neither factor is sufficient by itself.

Tests are unfair to minorities

To some extent this is true of all maximum-performance tests. The tests are based on the assumption that all people who take a test will be equally familiar or equally unfamiliar with the content matter. That is, the publisher must assume that all examinees will have had the same background of experience (including training). To the extent that the assumption is not true, the test will tend to favor some groups and to penalize others. Because tests usually are developed by upper-middle-class people who have upper-middle-class criteria in mind, the tests naturally tend to favor the upper-class and upper-middle-class groups.

Although this unfairness probably cannot be completely avoided, there are some tests on which the items are less "culturally loaded" than others. One difficulty with trying to eliminate items that are too culturally biased is that they are often ones which seem to relate best to job or school success.

Test bias has been a matter of some concern to major publishers for many years—and their diligence has certainly been enhanced by test critics. Every major publisher now has full-time staff and/or consultants working to minimize test bias. Some tests are now available in a second language (usually Spanish).

Personnel workers will find assistance and guidance from the Equal Employment Opportunities Commission (EEOC) if needed. But school users of tests will need to exercise caution in all of their test interpretations with minority youth—if they are to minimize this criticism.

Intelligence tests do not measure creativity

No one has ever claimed that they do, but critics denounce intelligence tests for not measuring creativity. No intelligence test gets at all cognitive functions. One psychologist (J. P. Guilford) contends that there are at least 120 recognizably different intellective factors. Perhaps, indeed, there may be many more such factors that will be revealed by future research.

Intelligence tests starting with Binet (about 1905) have tended to be school related. Most present-day intelligence tests have a similar school orientation although some tests are slanted more toward use in an industrial personnel setting or in a clinical situation. Even for these latter uses, intelligence tests rarely include much that could be considered a measure of creativity.

We may question whether intelligence tests should measure creativity. What is creativity? There is far from universal agreement on the answer to that question. In fact, there is less agreement among various definitions of creativity than there is among definitions of intelligence. (And there are certainly different definitions for that concept!)

The dimension of creativity is an important one; however, until we have more evidence of the validity of creativity tests, we should not be too dismayed that intelligence tests do not measure it.

People use tests to label children as morons, etc.

Unfortunately people do sometimes misuse tests in this way. Tests are best viewed as sources of information. As such, they are appropriately used in helping with decisions by people and about people (as in making individual and institutional decisions).

It is morally indefensible, except in extreme or emergency situations, to use any single test as the basis for making a decision. In the clinical application, it is conceivable that a licensed psychologist might make a recommendation on the basis of a single test if the clinical signs were extreme enough to warrant it. In the school, a teacher or administrator might make a tentative placement on the basis of an achievement test. But both the psychologist and the educationist should be equally ready to reverse the decisions if behavior warrants. If the child (or adult) proves able to do the work, that individual should not be kept from doing the work because of some test score. Tests may reflect or predict ability; they do not cause ability!

> Harriet Hughes, a teacher in nearby Hume High School, is dismayed with what is happening to one of her students, Holly. Despite the fact that Holly has earned As in almost every course she has ever taken, the school counselor has insisted that she must not take the academic courses that would permit her to qualify for admission to college ". . . because Holly's tests show that she cannot do quality work in school."
> What can we do about such a situation? In the first place, of course, we must evaluate its credibility—is it true? Are there circumstances that modify its accuracy? Beyond that, a concerned person can try to correct the condition. In Holly's case, I called an official at the Board of Education; she, in turn, arranged for a counseling supervisor to go to the school and review proper test use with all the counselors at the school. Holly's case will be discussed with Holly's counselor to see whether the girl should be permitted to take higher-level work.

Along somewhat similar lines, I have heard people criticize maximum-performance tests because they have helped a person form a low self-concept. True, but concepts of self and of others will be formed even in the absence of any testing. The emphasis should be placed, I feel, on the correct interpretation of test results. There is no place for the assertions that tests *prove* that one has little ability, that one has too little ability to go to college, and the like. Tests do not prove any such thing. In the extreme, they may reflect the fact that a person has limited ability. Even in extreme cases, however, the skilled test interpreter will allow a generous margin for possible error.

Test debunkers seem to forget two things: mistakes in classification are made (and have often been made in the past) without the aid of tests; and tests sometimes reveal ability that nontest sources have denied. For example:

> Newspapers and magazines report occasionally an elderly man (or, less often, an elderly woman) being released from years of confinement in an institution for the mentally retarded. Years before, these stories go, a child considered stupid by his parents or his teacher was admitted to the institution. Now, after testing has revealed that he is not markedly deficient, he is being released from confinement.
> In school settings, something similar happens from time to time. A test may reveal that the pupil has much more mental ability than either teacher or parents had thought.

Standardized tests favor the glib and penalize the thoughtful

This line of reasoning argues that standardized tests (usually multiple-choice tests) give extra advantage to the person who can come up with a quick, superficial response. They penalize the person who is capable of more thoughtful analysis of the questions.

Although some multiple-choice questions deserve this criticism, it is no more generally true than the charge that essay examinations favor the fast writer. There is ample evidence that good multiple-choice items may demand reasoning, interpretation, and other high-level processes. As the late Professor D. G. Paterson, of the University of Minnesota, used to say: "Short-answer questions, such as the multiple-choice, demand that the instructor substitute a skill in writing good items for a skill in grading items."

Tests invade privacy

This criticism has usually been leveled against personality tests that are used in a nonclinical setting. The individual in counseling should be at the least as interested as the tester in revealing whatever can be revealed by the test. When criminal matters are involved, the privacy of the individual may be of less importance than other considerations.

But there is real question in the minds of many about whether the required use of personality tests in school, in employment, in civil and military government service, and so on, is justifiable. Does the school have a right to invade the privacy of its students? If so, under what conditions? All students, or just some?

In my opinion, the routine personality testing of students is not advisable. I don't believe it is ordinarily worth the time and the expense. In the school setting, I am less concerned with the issue of whether the school has the right to give such tests, for—as any school teacher knows—students reveal themselves in many ways, from the "show and tell" session of the primary pupils to the compositions and themes of the secondary students.

The information that is likely to be obtained from routine personality testing is not, in my opinion, worthwhile. I might feel differently if more schools had sufficient personnel skilled in the handling of personality test results. But there are too many false positives and false negatives (that is, misleading results), which require test sophistication in handling. Unless one knows how to deal with personality test results, an examiner may be likely to find disturbances where there are none and overlook youngsters who really do have disturbances.

Add to these objections the fact that parents may resent the personality tests, and I believe that we have compelling arguments against their routine use. But school psychologists and others *with adequate test training* should be allowed to use such tests in the study of individual children. Such an application, of course, is consistent with clinical usage.

I have less definite feelings about the issue of personality tests in government or private employment. There is at least some freedom of choice on the part of the examinee—although refusal to take the test may mean that the individual must choose not to compete for the position(s) available.

Should a private employer have the right to require an applicant for work to take a personality test? All applicants, or just ones about which there are "doubts"? After all, the employer may invest considerable time and money in training a new worker. Beyond that, the employer has a business to operate. Is it unreasonable to want to get the best possible employees—employees who are likely to do good work? May the employer not be concerned also with his future employees' ability to get along with co-workers, customers or clients, and the like?

Or, viewed differently, does the employer have any right to pry into an applicant's feelings and values? Should an employer be allowed to reject an applicant because he gives "different" responses to personality test items? Should he be allowed to reject the nonconformists? We now have laws to protect against certain discriminatory hiring practices (for example, on the basis of sex or race). Should the employer be permitted to safeguard the image of his company by requiring applicants for work to take personality tests?

Tests are not the only vehicles for getting at personal information, of course. There are other means such as the application blank and the interview.

> I once completed an application blank that asked whether I "use tobacco in any form?", "use alcohol in any form?", or would "be willing to teach Sunday School?"

I believe that employers should have some voice in the selection of their employees and that they may legitimately use personality tests; however, the user may be called upon to demonstrate the test's validity.

In summary, I believe that personality tests, when used unwisely, do constitute an unfair invasion of privacy; however, I think that they can be helpful in a wide variety of applications when interpreted by licensed psychologists.

Tests give changing results

Naturally—and for many reasons—tests give changing results. Tests are not perfect. Neither are other evaluative methods: the personal interview, the rating scale, direct observation, and so on. One should not evaluate any test against a criterion of perfection—only against other possible techniques. If a test gives useful information that we would not otherwise have, and does so without prohibitive cost, the test would seem desirable.

Also, individuals change over time. We may reasonably expect that test results will change along lines similar to the ways in which people change. And remember, people change in knowledge, in skills, in personality characteristics. They also change in the motivation they bring to the testing room at different times.

Under the best conditions, test results show some variation. It has always seemed strange to me that a person whose bowling score may vary by 40 to 50 points from one string to the next expresses surprise at hearing that someone's IQ has changed by ten to fifteen points over several years when tested with different tests.

Always remember that standard error of measurement!

Tests are misused and misinterpreted

I could not agree more completely with any statement!

The remedy lies, however, through better education in testing—rather than in the abolition of tests. We have substantial evidence that tests do sometimes help in some situations. Let's concentrate on how tests can be used more intelligently and more efficiently, so that we can get more true meaning (and less nonsense) out of the test results.

How? I have no magical formula, but I do think that a better under-standing of tests can be sought at all levels:

1. Test publishers can be encouraged to continue their good work in trying to make test manuals and materials readable and intelligible. They need con-stantly to remember, also, to remind test users of the practical shortcomings of tests.
2. School and business administrators need to insist that their respective person-nel offices use their tests wisely and employ suitable safeguards to keep tests, test equipment, and test results secure. Test results should be available only to the individual tested and to qualified personnel. When appropriate, admin-istrators should encourage or support in-service training on what test scores mean.
3. Counselors, guidance workers, school psychologists, personnel workers, and the like should take time occasionally to review the manuals of the tests they use, to restudy test statistics, and to look at new tests. Such people should plan occasional in-service training efforts to instruct individuals who receive test results about the meaning of test scores.
4. Teachers, foremen, and others who may have easy or natural access to test results should be encouraged to learn what they can about the nature of tests and test results. We should require training in test interpretation of all people whose positions involve the use of test results.
5. All interested adults should be encouraged to read about tests, their strengths and their limitations. There is a shortage of good material for general read-ing, but plenty of irresponsible nonsense poured out by less-than-fully-informed writers. An occasional PTA meeting might be devoted to explana-tions of tests and testing.
6. School children can be trained to be somewhat sophisticated about the mean-ing of test results. They have already learned to inquire about time limits and whether tests are "corrected for guessing" whenever they take standardized tests. Why not give them some measurement theory in their mathematics? Or a bit about evaluation and assessment in their social studies? Or something about the fallibility of observation in their sciences? Such efforts could, within a very short time, bring school children to a point of being able to recognize the strengths and weaknesses of standardized tests.

There is nothing wrong with most tests that educating the consumer cannot cure.

11 ‖ CONCLUDING REMARKS

Here are some of the more important principles for the new tester to bear in mind:

Know the Test

There is no substitute for knowledge of the test that is being given. Test titles are not always descriptive of the actual test content; furthermore, many terms can be defined differently by different people. The underlying rationale of a test may be very important to our understanding of it. Our interpretation of test results may differ for power and speeded tests, for individual and group tests, and the like. We should study the manual of any test we plan to interpret. Whenever practicable, test *selection* should be made only by people with sufficient background in measurement to understand the technical data descriptive of the test.

Know the Norms

It is especially important for us to know what norms are being used. We cannot interpret adequately without understanding what group our test scores are being compared with. We may want to use several different norms groups when they are available. For example, we may want to compare a high school senior's scores with both high school seniors and college freshmen, or a person's aptitude test results with both applicants and present employees. In some situations, we may want to develop our own local norms.

Know the Score

It is always good to "know the score" in the colloquial sense of that term; however, here we are being literal. We need to know whether a given number is a standard score (and what kind), a percentile rank, a raw score, or something else. Fantastic misunderstandings can result from confusing the various metrics (for example, confusing percent correct and percentile ranks).

Know the Background

Test results do not tell the entire story, and we should not expect them to. We must consider *all* available information—whether or not it comes from a test.

Communicate Effectively

In many settings, we have to communicate test results to others. To get the interpretation across to an examinee, we must be certain to give all pertinent information. Examinees may very well resist accepting any interpretation that differs from their own conceptions of themselves. Several techniques that I have found helpful are mentioned in Chapter 9.

Use the Test

Not too surprisingly, we can come to a better understanding of what a test is like by using it. As we develop more experience in working with tests, we can attempt some simple studies to see how well a particular test works for our own specific purposes. As we develop competence along research lines, we can have increased confidence in the interpretations.

Use Caution

Test scores reflect ability; they do not determine ability. Test scores may suggest, but never prove. We are much safer when we make interpretations based on the actual performance of those who have had similar scores (see expectancy tables on pages 57-59) than when we try to tell an examinee, "This score means that you will . . ."

Experts Still Needed

Testing can be very technical, and there are many subtleties not even hinted at in this book. There is still need for a testing specialist wherever tests are widely used. This specialist should be freely available to those who would like this assistance.

For example, we have barely mentioned tests of typical performance. When properly used by qualified persons, typical-performance tests may give clues to the personality dynamics of both normal and disturbed people. Test interpretation demands skills and knowledge beyond those covered in this book (although a reasonable job of interpreting interest tests and some simple inventory-style personality tests should not be much beyond the competence of most readers).

Projective tests, certainly, should be interpreted only be licensed psychologists or suitably trained psychiatrists. The diversity of projective techniques is so great that some degree of training is needed in each of the specific techniques that the psychologist uses. Projective techniques are not parlor games or classroom exercises for the personal amusement of the tester.

Even with tests of maximum performance, there are some areas which are best left to the expert. Individual tests of intelligence, for example, require special training of the examiner. The trained examiner should be the one, too, to report the results of individual intelligence tests, for the report should include much more than a mere test score; otherwise, the situation does not require the use of an individual test in the first place.

We have mentioned almost nothing about exceptional children. Although much that has been said about testing applies equally well to them, there is much that does not. Special skills and understandings are demanded when we test these children.

The child with a language handicap cannot be tested fairly on a verbal test. Children who are hard of hearing or visually handicapped are similarly at a disadvantage when taking tests. And children with other handicaps or behavior problems may experience greater difficulty on tests than do "normal" children.

Exceptional children often have been assigned to special schools or to special classes. In such classrooms, they have been taught by teachers with special qualifications (special education teachers for the most part). Federal legislation first implemented in 1977 now decrees that such children must be taught in the least restrictive classrooms that are appropriate. This means that efforts will be made to *mainstream* them in "regular" classrooms.

Thus, regular classroom teachers, counselors, and the like may need to become more involved in the testing of (and test interpretation with) exceptional children. Extra knowledge and special skills are involved. Consult the testing expert whenever possible to see that the children receive fair treatment.

Throughout this book, we have considered briefly some implications of testing for guidance and counseling. On the other hand, we have recognized that the most effective use of tests in guidance and counseling situations requires much more knowledge than can be acquired solely from this book. There is a need for professional counselors and guidance workers— people who can extract the fullest meaning from test results and employ this meaning in their interviews.

Experts in tests and measurements are needed also to construct and validate new tests, to conduct research with tests, to advance measurement theory, and so on.

There should be at least one top-flight test specialist within each school system, each college, and each large industrial corporation. This specialist and his staff should have such varied duties as the following:

1. Keeping up to date on theoretical measurement; there is some excellent work being done that has not yet trickled down to the test user.
2. Maintaining a file of tests, both old and new, which might be consulted by other professional workers; this file would include manuals and catalogs.
3. Maintaining a library of books and periodical publications on tests and measurements.
4. Directing any major research activity involving tests.
5. Serving as advisor or consultant to people in the organization who want to do their own test-related research.
6. Evaluating new tests for possible use within the organization.
7. Selecting new tests for use within the organization.
8. Preparing local norms for tests.
9. Discussing test-related problems, issues, and questions with interested personnel both within and outside the organization.
10. Conducting in-service training programs for all people in the organization who work with tests.
11. Maintaining contact with governmental agencies concerned with tests and testing.
12. Serving as a liaison with test publishers—informing them of any difficulties with tests and staying current with publisher plans.

So many tests are available that experts are needed to evaluate them, and to select those which best meet the demands of their local situations. There is need for someone who can serve as a resource person for all those who use tests within an organization.

The ever-increasing governmental interest in *responsible* test-usage would seem to demand that every agency/institution using tests in the employment of large numbers of employees have such an authority available full-time to keep apprised of governmental regulations and changes. Most smaller organizations may find it more economical to retain an industrial or consulting psychologist to perform similar services.

The next few years are going to see numerous changes in policies. Some will come as various agencies acquire more experience and expertise. Others will come through court decisions. In my opinion, most governmental workers try to be fair to all concerned: examinee, company, and the public; however, agencies still have personnel who themselves are not knowledgeable about tests.

One recent issue of *The Industrial Psychologist* relates the story of two (hypothetical, we hope!) companies using the same test for employment selection. Validity studies at the companies yielded identical validity coefficients between test score and production on the job. But the smaller company was found guilty of discrimination and eventually was forced out of business, while the larger company was found innocent of discriminatory policies.

Why? Simply because of the difference in number of people tested at the two companies! (Larger values of a correlation coefficient are needed for statistical significance when the number of people involved is small.)

Go Ahead and Try!

I hope that I have been able to communicate to you some of the enthusiasm I feel about psychological and educational testing. I find this field of work fascinating. It's dynamic, and it's challenging. It is criticized, and it is challenged. One of my fondest hopes is that some readers will "catch" my enthusiasm and decide to specialize in psychometrics.

There are many pitfalls to the use of tests and their proper interpretation. There are all sorts of limitations to tests and to test scores. But tests *can* be helpful. Do not be overly cautious or you will never get any testing done. Go ahead and try!

DIRECTIONS FOR USING CONVERSION TABLE (pages 152-57)

This table may be used to convert from one derived-score system to another, assuming a normal distribution. Enter the table with the score in which you are interested; all entries on the same line are its normal-curve equivalents. **Care must be taken when using the table to compare results from different tests, for different norms groups are likely to be involved.**

See even pages of table for an explanation of symbols.

To use this Conversion Table for types of score *not* shown here, follow these steps:

FOR A LINEAR STANDARD SCORE (TYPE II A):

1. Find the amount by which an examinee's raw score differs from the mean of the group with which you wish to compare the examinee (either from the manual or from the local testing); i.e., $X - \overline{X}$.
2. Obtain the examinee's z-score by dividing this difference by the standard deviation of the same group; i.e., $(X - \overline{X})/s$.
3. Enter this value of z in the first column; all other entries on the same line are linear standard score equivalents (except for the percentile rank in the final column).

FOR A NORMALIZED STANDARD SCORE (TYPE II B 5):

1. Follow the directions for computing a percentile rank (*see* pages 152-57).
2. Enter this value of percentile rank in the extreme-right-hand column of the table. All other entries on the same line of the table are now *normalized* standard-score equivalents.

Customarily, none of these scores (except z) is expressed with a decimal. As a final step, therefore, you will usually round your score to the nearest whole number.

Do not use this table to find IQ equivalents unless "general population" norms are used.

Conversion Table for Derived Scores*

z $\left(\frac{X - \bar{X}}{s}\right)$ [Type II A 1][a]	T[b] (10z+50) [Type II A2 or II B 5 a][a]	AGCT (20z+100) [Type II A 3][a]	CEEB (100z+500) [Type II A 4][a]	IQ	
				Wechsler (15z+100) [Type II A 5 a][a]	Stanford-Binet (16z+100) [Type II A 5 b][a]
3.00	80	160	800	145	148
2.95	79.5	159	795	144	147
2.90	79	158	790	144	146
2.85	78.5	157	785	143	146
2.80	78	156	780	142	145
2.75	77.5	155	775	141	144
2.70	77	154	770	141	143
2.65	76.5	153	765	140	142
2.60	76	152	760	139	142
2.55	75.5	151	755	138	141
2.50	75	150	750	138	140
2.45	74.5	149	745	137	139
2.40	74	148	740	136	138
2.35	73.5	147	735	135	138
2.30	73	146	730	135	137
2.25	72.5	145	725	134	136
2.20	72	144	720	133	135
2.15	71.5	143	715	132	134
2.10	71	142	710	132	134
2.05	70.5	141	705	131	133
2.00	70	140	700	130	132
1.95	69.5	139	695	129	131
1.90	69	138	690	129	130
1.85	68.5	137	685	128	130
1.80	68	136	680	127	129
1.75	67.5	135	675	126	128
1.70	67	134	670	126	127
1.65	66.5	133	665	125	126
1.60	66	132	660	124	126
1.55	65.5	131	655	123	125
1.50	65	130	650	123	124
1.45	64.5	129	645	122	123
1.40	64	128	640	121	122
1.35	63.5	127	635	120	122
1.30	63	126	630	120	121
1.25	62.5	125	625	119	120
1.20	62	124	620	118	119
1.15	61.5	123	615	117	118
1.10	61	122	610	117	118
1.05	60.5	121	605	116	117

Stanine[c] [Type II B 5 b][a]	C-Score[c] [Type II B 5 c][a]	Sten[c] [Type II B 5 d][a]	Percentile rank [Type II B 2][a]
			99.9
			99.8
			99.8
			99.8
			99.7
			99.7
			99.6
	10		99.6
			99.5
			99.5
			99.4
			99.3
9		10	99.2
	—		99.1
			98.9
			98.8
			98.6
			98.4
			98.2
			98.0
			97.7
	9	5	97.4
			97.1
			96.8
			96.4
			96.0
			95.5
—	—	9	95.0
			94.5
			93.9
			93.3
			92.6
8	8	—	91.9
			91.2
			90.3
—	—		89.4
			88.5
		8	87.5
7	7		86.4
			85.3

*See directions for use on page 151.

[a]Refers to the classification of scores developed for this book; see Chapter 6.

[b]Since this table assumes a normal distribution, these values of T may be either T-scores (Type II A 2) or T-scaled scores (Type II B 5 a); if the distribution were not normal, T-scaled score entries would differ.

[c]This score takes only a very limited number of different values; therefore, it will have the same value for a range of values on other scores.

Conversion Table for Derived Scores (Continued)*

z $\left(\dfrac{X-\bar{X}}{s}\right)$	T[b] (10z+50)	AGCT (20z+100)	CEEB (100z+500)	IQ Wechsler (15z+100)	IQ Stanford-Binet (16z+100)
1.00	60	120	600	115	116
0.95	59.5	119	595	114	115
0.90	59	118	590	114	114
0.85	58.5	117	585	113	114
0.80	58	116	580	112	113
0.75	57.5	115	575	111	112
0.70	57	114	570	111	111
0.65	56.5	113	565	110	110
0.60	56	112	560	109	110
0.55	55.5	111	555	108	109
0.50	55	110	550	108	108
0.45	54.5	109	545	107	107
0.40	54	108	540	106	106
0.35	53.5	107	535	105	106
0.30	53	106	530	104	105
0.25	52.5	105	525	104	104
0.20	52	104	520	103	103
0.15	51.5	103	515	102	102
0.10	51	102	510	102	102
0.05	50.5	101	505	101	101
0.00	50	100	500	100	100
−0.05	49.5	99	495	99	99
−0.10	49	98	490	98	98
−0.15	48.5	97	485	98	98
−0.20	48	96	480	97	97
−0.25	47.5	95	475	96	96
−0.30	47	94	470	96	95
−0.35	46.5	93	465	95	94
−0.40	46	92	460	94	94
−0.45	45.5	91	455	93	93
−0.50	45	90	450	93	92
−0.55	44.5	89	445	92	91
−0.60	44	88	440	91	90
−0.65	43.5	87	435	90	90
−0.70	43	86	430	90	89
−0.75	42.5	85	425	89	88
−0.80	42	84	420	88	87
−0.85	41.5	83	415	87	86
−0.90	41	82	410	87	86
−0.95	40.5	81	405	86	85

Stanine[c]	C-Score[c]	Sten[c]	Percentile Rank
		—	84.1
			82.9
7	7		81.6
			80.2
		7	78.8
—	—		77.3
			75.8
			74.2
			72.6
			70.9
6	6	—	69.2
			67.4
			65.5
			63.7
			61.8
—	—	6	59.9
			57.9
			56.0
			54.0
			52.0
5	5	—	50.0
			48.0
			46.0
			44.0
			42.1
—	—	5	40.1
			38.2
			36.3
			34.5
			32.6
4	4	—	30.8
			29.1
			27.4
			25.8
			24.2
—	—	4	22.7
			21.2
			19.8
			18.4
3	3		17.1

*See directions for use on page 151.

[a]Refers to the classification of scores developed for this book; see Chapter 6.

[b]Since this table assumes a normal distribution, these values of T may be either T-scores (Type II A 2) or T-scaled scores (Type II B 5 a); if the distribution were not normal, T-scaled score entries would differ.

[c]This score takes only a very limited number of different values; therefore, it will have the same value for a range of values on other scores.

Conversion Table for Derived Scores (Continued)*

z_a $\left(\dfrac{X - \bar{X}}{s}\right)$	T[b] $(10z+50)$	AGCT $(20z+100)$	CEEB $(100z+500)$	IQ Wechsler $(15z+100)$	IQ Stanford-Binet $(16z+100)$
−1.00	40	80	400	85	84
−1.05	39.5	79	395	84	83
−1.10	39	78	390	84	82
−1.15	38.5	77	385	83	82
−1.20	38	76	380	82	81
−1.25	37.5	75	375	81	80
−1.30	37	74	370	81	79
−1.35	36.5	73	365	80	78
−1.40	36	72	360	79	78
−1.45	35.5	71	355	78	77
−1.50	35	70	350	78	76
−1.55	34.5	69	345	77	75
−1.60	34	68	340	76	74
−1.65	33.5	67	335	75	74
−1.70	33	66	330	75	73
−1.75	32.5	65	325	74	72
−1.80	32	64	320	73	71
−1.85	31.5	63	315	72	70
−1.90	31	62	310	72	70
−1.95	30.5	61	305	71	69
−2.00	30	60	300	70	68
−2.05	29.5	59	295	69	67
−2.10	29	58	290	69	66
−2.15	28.5	57	285	68	66
−2.20	28	56	280	67	65
−2.25	27.5	55	275	66	64
−2.30	27	54	270	66	63
−2.35	26.5	53	265	65	62
−2.40	26	52	260	64	62
−2.45	25.5	51	255	63	61
−2.50	25	50	250	63	60
−2.55	24.5	49	245	62	59
−2.60	24	48	240	61	58
−2.65	23.5	47	235	60	58
−2.70	23	46	230	60	57
−2.75	22.5	45	225	59	56
−2.80	22	44	220	58	55
−2.85	21.5	43	215	57	54
−2.90	21	42	210	57	54
−2.95	20.5	41	205	56	53
−3.00	20	40	200	55	52

Stanine[c]	C-Score[c]	Sten[c]	Percentile rank
		—	15.9
			14.7
			13.6
			12.5
			11.5
—	—		10.6
		3	9.7
			8.8
			8.1
			7.4
2	2	—	6.7
			6.1
			5.5
			5.0
			4.5
—	—	2	4.0
			3.6
			3.2
			2.9
			2.6
	1	2	2.3
			2.0
			1.8
			1.6
			1.4
	—		1.2
			1.1
			0.9
			0.8
			0.7
1		1	0.6
			0.5
			0.5
			0.4
	0		0.4
			0.3
			0.3
			0.2
			0.2
			0.2
			0.1

*See directions for use on page 151.

[a]Refers to the classification of scores developed for this book; see Chapter 6.

[b]Since this table assumes a normal distribution, these values of T may be either T-scores (Type II A 2) or T-scaled scores (Type II B 5 a); if the distribution were not normal, T-scaled score entries would differ.

[c]This score takes only a very limited number of different values; therefore, it will have the same value for a range of values on other scores.

APPENDIX

GLOSSARY OF TERMS

This glossary is intended primarily for readers who have had little formal training in testing. Because most of the terms are discussed elsewhere in the book, I have kept these definitions brief. The designation of various derived scores according to Types refers to the classification presented in Chapter 6.

accountability: (1) The state or condition of being responsible for those actions and behaviors and performances that are expected of a person because of the office or job held by that person. (2) Being held responsible or liable for performing duties of one's office or job.

achievement battery: A battery of achievement tests. (See *battery*.)

achievement test: A test designed to measure the amount of knowledge and/or skill a person has acquired, usually as a result of classroom instruction; may be either informal or standardized.

adjustment inventory: (See *personality test*.)

age equivalent: The chronological age for which a specified raw score is the average raw score.

age norms: Norms that give age equivalents for raw-score values.

age score: (See *age equivalent*.)

alternate-form reliability: A method of estimating test reliability by correlating two equivalent or parallel forms of the test.

anchor: A test or other variable used to ensure the comparability of two or more forms or editions or levels of a given instrument.

aptitude: That combination of characteristics, both native and acquired, which indicates the capacity of a person to develop proficiency in some skill or subject matter after relevant training; usually, but not necessarily, implies intellectual or skill aspects rather than emotional or personality characteristics.

articulation: Act or process of developing different editions, forms, and (especially) levels of the same test to yield results that are comparable.

assessment: Act or process of determining the present level (usually of achievement) of a group or individual.

average: General term for any central tendency measure; e.g., the mean, median, or mode.

battery: (1) A set of tests standardized on the same group, so that the results will be comparable; such a battery is called *integrated*. (2) A set of tests administered at about the same time to an individual or group; e.g., an employment battery or a counseling battery.

Buckley Amendment: A federal law passed in 1974 that decrees (among other provisions) that school records, including test data, must be made available to students and/ or parents upon request. Also called Educational Amendment Act of 1974 or Federal Family Educational Rights and Privacy Act of 1974.

Buros, Oscar K.:   Editor of the Mental Measurements Yearbooks, the "Bible" of testing.

C-score: A normalized standard score [Type II B 4 (c)] of eleven units.

chronological age (CA):   Any person's age; i.e., the length of time one has lived. The CA is a factor to consider when interpreting certain types of scores, especially age scores.

class interval: The unit of a frequency distribution, especially when the unit is greater than one; a band of score values assumed to be equal for purposes of computation or graphing.

coefficient of correlation: An index number indicating the degree of relationship between two variables; i.e., the tendency for values of one variable to change systematically with changes in values of a second variable; no relationship $= 0.00$, a perfect relationship $= \pm 1.00$. [Although there are different coefficients for various purposes, the basic type is the Pearson product-moment correlation (r), which is used when both variables are continuous, distributed symmetrically, etc.]

cognitive factors: Those characteristics of the individual that imply intellectual ability as contrasted with affective or personality characteristics.

composite score: A total score that consists of the sum of scores on two or more variables; (less commonly) an average of such scores.

concurrent validity: Criterion-related validity when both test scores and criterion values are obtained at about the same time.

construct validity: Test validation based on a combination of logical and empirical evidence of the relationship between the test and a related theory; concerned with the psychological meaningfulness of the test.

content-referenced: (1) Describes a test on which scores are interpreted directly in terms of performance on some achievement continuum (e.g., "can type 55 words per minute"). (2) *Syn* criterion-referenced.

content reliability: The consistency with which a test measures whatever it measures; may be estimated by a reliability coefficient based on (a) split halves, (b) alternate forms, or (c) internal consistency.

content validity: *Logical* evidence that the item content of a test is suitable for the purpose for which the test is to be used; concept is used principally with achievement tests.

continuous variable: A variable capable, actually or theoretically, of assuming any value—as opposed to a discrete variable, which may take only whole-number values; test scores are treated as being continuous, although they are less obvious examples than time, distance, weight, etc.

convergent thinking: Refers to a test that is scored for the "right" or "best" answer; used in opposition to divergent thinking.

correction-for-guessing formula: A formula sometimes used in scoring objective tests to make an allowance for items that have been "guessed" correctly; general formula is $X_c = R - (W/A - 1)$, where $X_c =$ corrected score, $R =$ number of items right, $W =$ number of items wrong, and $A =$ number of alternative choices per item. Although the underlying reasoning is dubious, the formula has considerable merit when examinees differ greatly in number of items left unanswered; use of the formula does not change order of scores when no one omits any items.

correlation: Tendency for two (or occasionally more) variables to change values concomitantly. Note: evidence of correlation is not evidence of causation. (See *coefficient of correlation*.)

creativity: (See *divergent thinking*.)

criterion (plural, **criteria**):   A standard against which a test may be validated; e.g., grade-point average is an obvious criterion for a scholastic aptitude test.

criterion-keying: Act or process of developing a scoring key empirically by noting differences in answers made by contrasting groups.

criterion-referenced: (1) Testing that is not *norms*-referenced, but where test performance is described directly in terms of performance at any given level on the continuum of an external variable. (2) *Syn.* content-referenced.

criterion-related validity: Test validity based on a correlation coefficient between test scores and criterion values. *Syn.* empirical validity.

cross-cultural test: A test believed to be suitable for use in different societies because it is relatively free from cultural influences (such as language).

cross validation: Act or process of verifying results obtained on one group (or one study) by replication with a different, but similar, group (or study).

culture-biased: Describes a test on which the items, whether intentionally or not, are easier for one cultural subgroup than for another or others; *culture-fair* describes a test that is relatively unbiased; no test can be completely culture-free.

curriculum validity: See *content validity*.

cutting score: The minimum passing score, usually determined through research, for some practical situation (e.g., college entrance or job selection). *Syn.* cutoff score.

decile: Any one of nine percentile points that divides a distribution into ten subgroups of equal frequency; e.g., the fifth decile (D_5) is the same as P_{50} or the median.

decile rank: A derived score (Type II B 5) expressed in terms of the nearest decile.

derived score: Any type of score other than a raw score.

deviation: The amount by which a score differs from a specified reference point (usually, but not always, the mean or other average).

deviation IQ: (1) A standard score (Type II A 5) with a mean fixed statistically at 100 and standard deviation fixed by the test's author; has advantages over the ratio IQ, which it is designed to approximate. (2) A normalized standard score [Type II B 4 (e)] designed to resemble a ratio IQ, but possessing certain advantages. (3) Rarely, derived score (Type IV C) in which IQ is equal to 100 plus the amount by which an examinee's raw score deviates from the norm for his age.

diagnostic test: (1) A test (usually of achievement) designed to identify specific educational difficulties. (2) A test given in connection with counseling or psychotherapy as an aid in determining the nature of an individual's mental disorder, maladjustment, etc.

difficulty value: A statement of a test item's difficulty, usually expressed as the percentage of individuals in a group who answer the item correctly.

discrete value: A value obtained through counting rather than measuring; thus, can take only whole-number values—e.g., number of students in each classroom—unlike continuous variables, which can assume any value.

discrimination value: Any statistic used to express the extent to which a test item shows a difference between high-ability and low-ability examinees.

distracter: Any incorrect alternative in a multiple-choice item.

distribution: (See *frequency distribution; normal distribution*.)

divergent thinking: Refers to a test in which novel or creative responses are desired; contrasts with the more-common convergent thinking tests.

domain-referenced measurement: (See *content-referenced*.)

edumetric: Measurement of learning outcomes through criterion-referenced measurement. Opposite of psychometric.

EEOC: Equal Employment Opportunity Commission.

empirical validity: (See *criterion-related validity*.)

equivalent form: Any of two or more forms of a test, usually standardized on the same population and published at the same time—designed to be similar in item content and difficulty so that scores on the forms will be similar.

error: A generic term for those elements in a test and testing situation that operate to keep a test from giving perfect results: (a) *constant errors* have a direct adverse effect on validity, but may not affect reliability (e.g., having arithmetic items in an English test); and (b) *variable* (or *random*) *errors* reduce reliability directly and validity indirectly (e.g., nonstandard conditions of test administration, chance passing or failing of items, ambiguous wording of test items). Note: errors are inherent in all measurement, but mistakes are not.

evaluation: A statement of test results that includes a judgmental factor (e.g., "The class is achieving higher than others in the school" or "Maria is doing better in arithmetic than in English").

expectancy table: Any table showing class intervals of test scores (or other predictor variable) along one axis and criterion categories (or similar information) along the other axis; entries show number or, more typically, percentage of individuals within specified score intervals who have achieved at given levels on the criterion variable.

extrapolation: Act or process of estimating values beyond those actually obtained; e.g., extreme values for both age and grade-placement scores have to be established in this manner.

face validity: Superficial appearance of validity; i.e., test looks as if it should measure what is intended.

factor: (1) Strictly and technically, an element or variable presumed to exist because of its ability to help explain some of the inter-relationships noted among a set of tests. (2) Equally properly, the ability or characteristic represented by a factor (definition 1). (3) Loosely, anything partially responsible for a result or outcome (e.g., "study is an important factor in obtaining good grades").

factor analysis: Any of several complex statistical procedures for analyzing the intercorrelations among a set of tests (or other variables) for the purpose of identifying the factors (definitions 1 and 2), preferably few in number, that cause the intercorrelations.

frequency: The number of individuals obtaining any specified score or falling in any specified class interval.

frequency distribution: Any orderly arrangement of scores, usually from highest to lowest, showing the frequency with which each score or each class interval occurs.

frequency polygon: A type of graph commonly used to portray a distribution of test scores (or values of some other continuous variable).

grade equivalent: (See *grade-placement score*.)

grade norm: The average test score for pupils with a given grade placement.

grade-placement score: A derived score (Type II D 2) expressed as the grade placement of those pupils for whom a given score was average.

heterogeneity: Possessing great variability; thus, in testing: a test with a great variety of content, or a group that varies considerably in the attribute tested. *Adj.* heterogeneous.

homogeneity: Having little variability; thus, in testing: a) a test composed of items that vary little in type or b) a group that varies little in the attribute tested. *Adj.* homogeneous.

individual test: A test that usually, if not always, can be administered to only one examinee at a time.

inferential statistics: Statistics used to test hypotheses, establish confidence limits, etc. (e.g., *t*, chi square, or analysis of variance).

informal test: Any test intended primarily for the use of the test constructor or in a single setting used in opposition to standardized tests.

intellectual status index: A derived score (Type III B), similar to a ratio IQ.

intelligence: An abstraction variously defined by different authorities; in general, the capacity or set of capacities that enables an individual to learn, to cope with the environment, to solve problems, etc.

intelligence quotient (IQ):   (See *deviation IQ; ratio IQ.*)

internal consistency: A term referring to any of several techniques for estimating the content reliability of a test through knowledge of item analysis statistics.

interpolation: Act or process of estimating a value that falls between two known or computed values; this practice is often followed in establishing age-and grade-placement scores, so that the norms table will cover all possible ages or grade placements.

inventory: (1) Most commonly used to describe a paper-and-pencil test of personality, interest, attitude, or the like. (2) Less commonly used to describe an achievement test designed to "take an inventory" of a student or class knowledge or skill on a specific task.

ipsative: A type of test or score in which a person's performance on one variable is influenced (usually inversely) by scores on one or more other variables within the same test.

item: (1) Any individual problem or question on a test. (2) Usually the basic unit to be scored on an objective test.

item analysis: The act or process of examining a test item empirically to determine (a) its difficulty value, and (b) its discrimination value. Note: such values will differ somewhat from group to group, from time to time, and according to the particular statistic used.

key, scoring: (1) The collection of correct answers (or scored responses) for the items of a test. (2) The device or sheet, containing the scored responses, which is used in scoring the test.

Kuder-Richardson formula: Any of several formulas developed by Kuder and Richardson for estimating content reliability by internal-consistency analysis.

local norms: Test norms that are based on people tested locally (e.g., by a school system or industry) in the hope that the norms may give more or better information than is provided by the publisher in the test manual.

machine scoring: Act or process of scoring a test with the aid of a mechanical or electrical device that counts and may record the scored responses of a test (or subtest); the most common machines involve one or more of these processes: (a) mark sensing, (b) punched hole, or (c) electronic scanning.

mark sensing: Descriptive of a system of machine scoring tests that uses an electrical contact to "sense" responses to be scored.

mastery testing: Content-referenced measurement aimed at assessing degree of accomplishment of a stated skill.

maximum-performance test: Any test on which the examinee is directed, at least implicitly, to do the best job he can; e.g., intelligence, aptitude, and achievement tests. *Ant.* typical-performance test.

mean: Most widely used measure of central tendency; equals the sum of scores divided by the number of examinees.

median: Next to the mean, the most common measure of central tendency; the point on the scale of score values which separates the group into two equal subgroups; the fiftieth percentile (P_{50}), the second quartile (Q_2), and the fifth decile (D_5).

mental age: A derived score [Type II D 1(a)] *See* page 103-5.

modal age: The chronological age that is most typical of children with a given grade placement in school.

modal-age norms: Norms based only on those pupils near the modal age for their actual grade placement.

mode: A measure of central tendency; that score value which has the highest frequency; i.e., that score obtained by more examinees than any other.

N: Symbol for the number of examinees in any specified group.

NCE (normal curve equivalent):   A normalized standard score with a mean of 50.00 and a standard deviation of 21.06; intended for research use only.

norm: Average, normal, or standard for a group of specified status (e.g., of a given age or grade placement).

normal distribution (curve):   A useful mathematical model representing the distribution expected when an infinite number of observations (e.g., scores) deviate from the mean only by chance; although a normal distribution can never be attained in reality, many actual distributions do approach this model. The curve drawn to portray the normal distribution is a symmetrical bell-shaped curve whose properties are completely known. See Chapter 4.

normalized standard score: Any of several scores (Type II B) that resemble standard scores (Type II A), but which are computed like percentile ranks.

norms: A set of values descriptive of the performance on a test of some specified group; usually shown as a table giving equivalent values of some derived score for each raw score on the test.

objective test: A test for which the scoring procedure is specified completely in advance, thereby permitting complete agreement among different scorers.

omnibus test: A test, usually of intelligence, in which items of many different types are used in obtaining a single overall score; usually has one set of directions and one overall time limit.

paper-and-pencil test: Any test which requires no materials other than paper, pencil, and test booklet; most group tests are paper-and-pencil tests.

parameter: A summary or descriptive value (e.g., mean or standard deviation) for a population or universe; i.e., a parameter is to a population as a statistic is to a sample.

percentage-correct score: A derived score (Type I A) expressing the examinee's performance as a percentage of the maximum possible score.

percentile (P): Any of the 99 points along the scale of score values that divide a distribution into 100 groups of equal frequency; e.g., P_{73} is that point below which fall 73 percent of the cases in a distribution.

percentile rank (PR): A derived score (Type II B 2) stated in terms of the percentage of examinees in a specified group who fall below a given score point. *Syn.* centile rank.

performance test: An ambiguous term used variously to mean (a) a test involving special apparatus, as opposed to a paper-and-pencil test; (b) a test minimizing verbal skills; or (c) a work-sample test.

personality test: A typical-performance test, questionnaire, or other device designed to measure some affective characteristic of the individual.

population: Any entire group so designated; i.e., the total group that is of interest or concern. *Syn.* universe.

power test: Any maximum-performance test for which speed is not an important determinant of score; thus, a test with a very generous (or no) time limit.

predictive validity: Criterion-related validity where criterion values are obtained subsequent to the determination of the test scores.

probable error (PE): A measure of variability, rarely used today, found by multiplying 0.6745 by either the standard deviation (to obtain the probable error of a distribution) or the standard error (to obtain the probable error of some statistic).

profile: A graphic representation of the performance of an individual (or, less commonly, a group) on a series of tests, especially the tests in an integrated battery.

prognostic test: A test used to predict future performance (usually success or failure) in a particular task.

projective technique: Any method of personality measurement or study that makes use of deliberately ambiguous stimuli (e.g., ink blots, incomplete sentences, etc.) into which examinees "project" their personality when responding.

psychometric: Psychological measurement that is norms-referenced, rather than criterion-referenced. *Ant.* edumetric.

punched hole: Descriptive of a system of machine-scoring tests; utilizes holes punched into cards (e.g., IBM cards).

quartile: Any of the three points that divide a frequency distribution into four groups of equal frequency. The first quartile (Q_1) equals the twenty-fifth percentile (P_{25}); $Q_2 = P_{50}$ = median; and $Q_3 = P_{75}$.

r: Symbol for Pearson product-moment correlation coefficient.

random error: See *variable error.*

random sample: A sample drawn from a population in such a manner that each member has an equal chance of being selected; samples so drawn are unbiased and should yield statistics representative of the population.

range: The difference between highest and lowest scores made on a test.

ratio IQ: A derived score (Type III A), no longer in common use; the formula *100 (MA/ CA)*, where MA = mental age determined from a test, and CA = chronological age (adjusted for older adolescents and for adults).

raw score: The basic score initially obtained from scoring a test according to directions given by the test maker; usually equal to number of correct responses, but may be number of wrong answers or errors, time required for a task, etc.

reliability: Reproduce-ability of a set of scores under differing conditions; i.e., consistency or stability of a measuring instrument; necessary for, but not sufficient for, validity. Commonly expressed as a reliability coefficient or a standard error of measurement.

reliability coefficient: A coefficient of correlation designed to estimate a test's reliability by correlating (a) scores on equivalent forms, (b) scores on matched halves (corrected for length), or (c) scores on two administrations of same test.

reproduce-ability: See *reliability*, pages 31–37.

sample: A general term referring to a group, however selected, assumed to represent an entire population.

scaled score: (1) Loosely, any derived score. (2) More technically, any of several systems of scores (usually similar to standard scores) used in (a) articulating different forms, editions, and/or levels of a test; or (b) developmental research.

selection ratio: The ratio of number of persons selected to number of persons tested; other things being equal, lower ratios result in a higher proportion of those who succeed among those selected.

semi-interquartile range (quartile deviation, Q): A measure of variability equal to one-half the difference between the third quartile (P_{75}) and the first quartile (P_{25}); i.e., $Q = (Q_3 - Q_1)/2.$

sigma: Greek letter widely used in statistics. Capital sigma (Σ) means "to add" or "find the sum of." Lower case sigma (σ) is often used to mean standard deviation, especially of a population; however, s, rather than σ, has been used in this book.

skewed (distribution): A noticeably asymmetrical distribution of scores. A distribution with many high scores and very few low scores is said to be "skewed to the left" or "negatively skewed."

Spearman-Brown (prophecy) formula: A formula designed to estimate the reliability that a test will have if its length is changed and other factors remain constant; most commonly used in "correcting" split-half (i.e., "odd-even") reliability coefficients.

speed test: (1) A test on which an examinee's speed is an important determinant of his score. (2) A test on which the score equals the time taken to complete it.

split-half reliability coefficient: An estimate of content reliability based on the correlation between scores on two halves of a test; usually, the odd and even items are scored separately to provide these two half-test-length scores. Must not be used with a speed test. *See* Spearman-Brown.

standard deviation (s or σ): A measure of variability preferred over all others because of its soundness mathematically and its general usefulness as a basis for (a) standard scores, (b) standard errors, and (c) various statistical tests of significance.

standard error: An estimate of what the standard deviation of a statistic would be if successive values were found for that statistic through repeated testings (usually on different, but similar, samples drawn from the same population).

standard error of estimate: A standard deviation based on differences between obtained scores and scores predicted (from knowledge of correlation between a predictor variable and a criterion variable).

standard error of measurement: An estimate of the standard deviation that would be found in the distribution of scores for a specified person if that person were to be tested repeatedly on the same or similar test (assuming no learning).

standardization: Act or process of developing a standardized test; many stages are involved in careful standardization, among these are the following: tryout of items, item analyses, validation studies, reliability studies, development of norms, and the like.

standard score: Any of several derived scores (Type II A) based on number of standard deviations between a specified raw score and the mean of the distribution.

stanine: A normalized standard score [Type II B 4 (b)] of nine units, 1-9; in a normal distribution, stanines have a mean of 5.0 and a standard deviation of 1.96.

sten: A normalized standard score [Type II B 4 (d)], similar to the more common stanine, but having five units on either side of the mean; the mean sten (in a normal distribution) is 5.5, and the standard deviation is about 2.0.

stencil key: A scoring key made for placing over the answer sheet, the examinee's responses being visible either through holes prepared for that purpose or through the transparent material of the key itself.

strip key: A scoring key prepared in a column or strip which may be laid alongside a column of answers on the examinee's answer sheet or test paper; when several columns of answers are printed on the same scoring key, it becomes a "fan" or "accordion" key.

subjective test: A test on which the personal opinion or impression of the scorer is one determinant of the obtained score; i.e., the scoring key cannot be (or is not) fully prescribed in advance of scoring.

survey test: A test designed to measure achievement in one or more specified areas, usually with the intention of assessing group understanding—rather than individual measurement—of the concepts, principles, and facts.

T-scaled score: A normalized standard score [Type II B 4 (a)] with a mean of 50 and a standard deviation of 10.

T-score: A standard score (Type II A 2) having a mean of 50 and a standard deviation of 10.

temporal reliability: Test stability over a period of time, estimated through a test-retest reliability coefficient.

test security: Act or process of ensuring that only authorized people have access to tests and test supplies.

true score: A theoretical concept never obtainable in practice, an error-free score; usually defined as the average of the scores that would be obtained if a specified examinee were to take the same test an infinite number of times (assuming no learning).

truncated: Describes a distribution of scores that is cut off artificially or arbitrarily at some point, whatever the reason; e.g., a distribution in which some examinees receive the maximum possible score, thereby not enabling these examinees to score as high as they could have if the test had a suitable ceiling.

typical-performance test: Any test designed to measure what an examinee is "really like," rather than any intellectual or ability characteristic; e.g., tests of personality, attitude, interest, etc. *Ant.* maximum-performance test.

usability: That attribute which is concerned with such practical matters as cost of the test, time to administer and score, etc.

validity: The extent to which a test does the job desired of it; the evidence may be either empirical or logical. Unless otherwise noted, criterion-related validity is implied.

variability: The amount of scatter or dispersion in a set of scores.

variable: (1) Any trait or characteristic that may change with the individual or the observation. (2) More strictly, any representation of such trait or characteristic that is capable of assuming different values; e.g., a test is a variable.

variable error: Any deviation from a true score attributable to one or more nonconstant influences, such as guessing, irregular testing conditions, etc.; always has a direct adverse effect on reliability; by definition, variable errors are uncorrelated with true scores.

variance: A statistic, equal to the square of the standard deviation (s^2).

work-sample test: A test on which the examinee's response to a simulated on-the-job problem or situation is evaluated; e.g., a pre-employment typing test.

z-score: The basic standard score (Type II A); widely used in test-related research; $z = (X - \overline{X})/s$, where $\overline{X}$ = mean score, and s = standard deviation.

BIBLIOGRAPHY

The books listed below are only representative of the many excellent references that may prove valuable for those who wish to learn more about testing.

AHMANN, J. STANLEY AND MARVIN D. GLOCK, *Evaluating Pupil Growth* (6th ed.), Boston: Allyn & Bacon, 1980.

AIKEN, LEWIS R., JR., *Psychological Testing and Assessment* (5th ed.), Boston: Allyn & Bacon, 1985.

ANASTASI, ANNE, *Psychological Testing* (5th ed.), New York: Macmillan, 1982.

BROWN, FREDERICK G., *Principles of Educational and Psychological Testing* (2nd ed.), Hinsdale, IL: Dryden Press, 1976.

BUROS, OSCAR K., ED., *The Eighth Mental Measurements Yearbook,* Highland Park, NJ: Gryphon Press, 1978. Best single reference for both critical reviews of tests and bibliographic lists of studies using specific tests.

CHUN, KI-TAEK, *et. al., Measures for Psychological Assessment,* Ann Arbor: University of Michigan, 1975. A guide to 3,000 original sources of socio-psychological tests (many of them not thoroughly standardized).

CRONBACH, LEE J., *Essentials of Psychological Testing* (4th ed.), New York: Harper & Row, 1984.

CRONBACH, LEE J. AND GOLDINE GLESER, *Psychological Tests and Personnel Decisions* (2nd ed.), Urbana: University of Illinois Press, 1965.

CRONBACH, LEE., *et al., The Dependability of Behavioral Measurements,* New York: John Wiley, 1972.

DuBois, PHILIP H., *A History of Psychological Testing,* Boston: Allyn & Bacon, 1970.

EBEL, ROBERT L., *Essentials of Educational Measurement* (3rd ed.), Englewood Cliffs, NJ: Prentice-Hall, 1979.

EBEL, ROBERT L., *Practical Problems in Educational Measurement,* Lexington: Heath, 1980.

EQUAL EMPLOYMENT OPPORTUNITIES COMMISSION, *Job Discrimination? Laws and Rules You Should Know,* Washington, DC: EEOC, 1974.

EQUAL EMPLOYMENT OPPORTUNITIES COMMISSION, *The Uniform Guidelines on Employee Selection Procedures,* Washington, DC: EEOC, 1973.

GHISELLI, EDWIN E. *et al., Measurement Theory for the Behavioral Sciences,* San Francisco: W. H. Freeman, 1981.

GRAHAM, JOHN R. AND ROY S. LILLY, *Psychological Testing,* Englewood Cliffs, NJ: Prentice-Hall, 1984.

GUION, ROBERT M., *Personnel Testing,* New York: McGraw-Hill, 1965.

GULLIKSEN, HAROLD, *Theory of Mental Tests,* New York: John Wiley, 1950. Dated and difficult, but still a classic.

HOPKINS, KENNETH D. AND JULIAN STANLEY, *Educational and Psychological Measurement and Evaluation* (6th ed.), Englewood Cliffs, NJ: Prentice-Hall, 1981.

LEMKE, ELMER AND WILLIAM WIERSMA, *Principles of Psychological Measurement,* Boston: Houghton Mifflin, 1976.

LINDEMAN, RICHARD H. AND PETER F. MERENDA, *Educational Measurement* (2nd ed.), Glenview, IL: Scott, Foresman, 1979.

LORD, FREDERIC M. *Application of Item Response Theory to Practical Testing Problems,* Hillsdale, NJ: Erlbaum, 1980.

LORD, FREDERIC M. AND MELVIN R. NOVICK, *Statistical Theories of Mental Test Scores,* Reading, MA: Addison-Wesley, 1968.

LYMAN, HOWARD B., *Intelligence, Aptitude, and Achievement Testing,* Guidance Monograph Series III: Testing, Boston: Houghton Mifflin, 1968.

LYMAN, HOWARD B., "Metrics Used in Reporting Test Results," in *New Directions for Testing and Measurement* No. 6, ed. S. T. Mayo. San Francisco: Josey-Bass, 1980.

MCLAUGHLIN, KENNETH F., *Interpretation of Test Results,* Washington, DC: USGPO, 1964.

MEDAUS, GEORGE F., ED., *The Courts, Validity and Minimum Competency Testing,* Boston: Kluwer-Nijhoff, 1982.

MEHRENS, WILLIAM A. AND IRVIN J. LEHMANN, *Standardized Tests in Education* (3rd ed.), New York: Holt, Rinehart and Winston, 1980.

NOLL, VICTOR *et al., Introduction to Educational Measurement* (4th ed.), Boston: Houghton Mifflin, 1979.

NUNNALLY, JUM C., *Psychometric Theory* (2nd ed.), New York: McGraw-Hill, 1978.

SAMUDA, RONALD J., *Psychological Testing of American Minorities,* New York: Harper and Row, 1975.

SHAYCOFT, MARION F., *Handbook of Criterion-Referenced Testing: Development, Evaluation, and Use,* New York: Garland STPM Press, 1979.

SIEGEL, JEROME, *Personnel Testing Under EEO* (An AMA Research Study), New York: American Management Association, 1980.

Standards for Educational and Psychological Tests, Washington, DC: American Psychological Association, 1974; revised, 1985.

THORNDIKE, ROBERT L., *Personnel Selection,* New York: John Wiley, 1949. Old, but good.

THYNE, J. M., *Principles of Examining,* New York: John Wiley, 1974.

INDEX